THE Loneliness WORKBOOK

A Guide to Developing and Maintaining Lasting Connections

Mary Ellen Copeland, M.S., M.A.

New Harbinger Publications, Inc.

Publisher's Note

This publication is designed to provide accurate and authoritative information in regard to the subject matter covered. It is sold with the understanding that the publisher is not engaged in rendering psychological, financial, legal, or other professional services. If expert assistance or counseling is needed, the services of a competent professional should be sought.

Distributed in the U.S.A. by Publishers Group West; in Canada by Raincoast Books; in Great Britain by Airlift Book Company, Ltd.; in South Africa by Real Books, Ltd.; in Australia by Boobook; and in New Zealand by Tandem Press.

Cover design by Poulson/Gluck Design
Cover illustration by Edmund Nägele
Edited by Kayla Sussell
Text design by Michele Waters

Library of Congress Catalog Number: 99-75298
ISBN 1-57224-203-5 Paperback

New Harbinger Publications' Web site address: www.newharbinger.com

02   01   00

10   9   8   7   6   5   4   3   2

This book is dedicated to the memory of my dear friend and supporter Nancy Jane Post. Over the course of our twelve-year friendship we had lunch together at least 248 times. We had a pact never to leave a lunch without a date in our date books for our next time together. From the first lunch to the last, my time in the company of this great woman has sustained, fulfilled, and enriched my life.

Contents

Acknowledgments

Special thanks to Teta Hilsdon, Ed Anthes, Martha Bauman, and Jean Andrew for their valuable inspiration, assistance, and support; and to all the wonderful people who gave input by coming to a support group, filling out a lengthy questionnaire and/or responding to my queries for more information and guidance. Without them, this book would not have been possible.

Prelude

Loneliness is an old and ongoing human condition. Imagine the loneliness of people alone in the wilderness; of those who left their families and friends to explore and settle new lands; of those who have lost many or all of their loved ones through illness, aging, or disaster; of people who have a disability or disfigurement that causes others to avoid or scorn them; of people who have not been able to connect with others because they feel so self-conscious or have no idea of how to make such a connection.

Having friends, supporters, and emotional connections with others in our lives is vitally important. We know that being lovingly supported and supporting others are powerful contributors to our social, psychological, spiritual, and even physical well-being. Such support is most assuredly a powerful antidepressant. It makes us feel good. It gives us the motivation and courage to go on in even the hardest of times. It enriches our lives, making every experience feel better.

And yet in our fast-paced, technologically oriented and economically driven society, the importance of connection with others is given little or only superficial attention. The family, neighborhood, and community gatherings that were so common in the past have been replaced by television and the Internet and an increased perception of the need for privacy because of overpopulation and/or urban sprawl. Modern transportation systems and the automobile have made it easy for people to go far beyond their neighborhoods and communities for work and recreation. Families are working so hard to meet their expenses that they have little energy left over to be with each other in meaningful ways and to be supportive members of the communities in which they live. The focus in our schools is on academics, not on the development of social skills. When are we going to recognize that people's meaningful connections with others are a top priority?

I have wanted to explore how other people resolve the issue of loneliness in their lives for a very long time, for as long as I have been aware of how good it feels to be closely connected with others—and how terrible it feels to be alone and unsupported. I felt very alone and unsupported when I was a child. My mother left our household when I was eight years old. (She spent nine years in a state psychiatric hospital.) No one in the public schools I attended back then, in the late 1940s and early 1950s, was very concerned about the quiet little girl who didn't talk to anyone and didn't have any friends.

All of my teachers had about forty students in their classrooms and were grateful for a child who caused no trouble, didn't say anything, and was practically invisible.

I remember going with two former classmates to visit one of those teachers when I was older. She remembered them, but she didn't remember me. Many of my former classmates probably don't remember me either. My father had five children to deal with and he certainly didn't have time to worry about whether any of us had friends. He was busy making sure we had food on the table, clean clothes to wear, and that we stayed out of trouble. With long hours of work, he had little time even to help us learn how to connect with and support each other. So I moved through grade school, high school, and college with poor social skills, feeling lonely much of the time and having many of the attempts I made at connecting with others sputter out and eventually fail.

As an adult I have had much more success at relieving my deep loneliness. But these successes were achieved the hard way—through trial and error. This process took me through two ill-advised and abusive marriages and many relationships that were unsatisfactory at their best. I didn't know how to choose people to be with and whom to avoid. I didn't know how to make connections with good people or how to keep healthy connections strong. I was hurt, and I am sure that in my ignorance I hurt others. This book was written to try to help others avoid making the kinds of mistakes that I and many others have made while attempting to ease and relieve the loneliness in our lives.

One of the arenas in which I learned about the importance of having a strong circle of supporters was through my ongoing work of teaching and learning from people who are overcoming symptoms of serious emotional distress. These are symptoms that prevent them from becoming the kind of people they want to be and from doing the things they want to do with their lives. Although such extreme symptoms are not experienced by everyone, the information that I have gathered in my studies points to the need for *everyone* to have good social supports in place. When I began studying how people deal with deep depression and other severe emotional symptoms in the 1980s—in an effort to find out how to help myself feel better—I became aware that strong connection with and support from others is essential to healing, recovery, and ongoing health. I also learned that developing, sustaining, making good use of, and from time to time rebuilding a network of supporters to counteract loneliness is very hard work for many people.

When I began this research, I had been struggling for many years with deep depression and acute mania that had become severe and disabling. My life was not what I wanted it to be, but I felt as if it were totally out of my control. My research, which involved talking with other people to learn how they had relieved serious emotional symptoms and taken control of their lives, led me to understand the importance of strong emotional connections with others.

I took a close look at my situation. I was lonely much of the time. I depended too much on a few people for support. I was overly dependent on these few and sometimes the relationships were very one-sided—others provided me with support and I gave little back to them. Most of their time with me was spent taking care of my physical needs. Little time was left for them to listen to me, or for me to provide them with support, or to enjoy interesting activities together.

Because of this assessment I began to work on creating a change. I realized that most of my support came from my adult children. But they were busy starting families and building careers. I needed to widen my circle. Over the next few years I joined a support group for people with mood disorders. I became an active member of a women's support group and began going on informal hikes with small groups of people. I focused my attention on mutual support—being there for others as much as they were there for me, staying in touch with interesting people I met, attending interesting activities in the community and occasionally initiating fun activities (this was hard for me). I also became an active peer counselor. I built into my weekly schedule at least one or two times when I could get together with a supporter and divide the time between us equally, listening and sharing without interruption. I learned to do these things better and better over time, and as I connected with more people, I learned even better skills. Committing myself to learning and to improving my life was an important early step.

The result of widening my circle of support is that, while I still have some difficulty managing extreme mood swings, they are much less frequent and much less intense. The quality of my life has improved significantly. I am much happier and healthier.

I still have to work at keeping my support system strong. Sometimes I don't feel like going to my support group. Most of the time I go anyway and I am always glad I did. If my mood is a little low, I call a close friend or get together with people I know will help me to feel better. In the past this was hard for me. But now, more and more often I just do it. And it always helps. I have a wide circle of close friends and it continues to widen. I keep in touch through phone calls, notes, email and, best of all, in person, doing fun things together.

Finally, at age fifty-eight, I am married to a wonderfully loving and supportive man. I have close connections with my adult children, stepchildren, and grandchildren, and I feel closer to my siblings than ever before. I have a large and expanding circle of loving friends who enrich my life. They are there with me through good times and hard times. I continue to belong to a women's support group that has been meeting every Monday night for more than ten years. I have also learned how to enjoy being by myself—and making that time rich and rewarding. Nowadays, I frequently find myself looking forward to and even relishing time spent alone. I like myself and my life a lot more than I used to. And I look forward to continued learning in the years to come.

Methodology

In writing this book I have drawn from my own life experience and from a research project in which I reached out to people who have willingly shared the thoughts, ideas, and actions that helped them to relieve the loneliness in their lives. These volunteers were recruited from my workshops, networking with my colleagues, and my Web site on the Internet. The key thing that I learned from all of them is that there is hope. You *can* change your life and shape it the way you want it to be.

The first step in the research process was to hold a focus group, a meeting of a diverse group of people. These people helped me define the questions to ask in a written survey. I then distributed the questionnaire to the volunteers. As I received their responses, I found that I wanted more specific information on some topics. I got this information through numerous interviews and an additional meeting of a focus group. It was an exciting process that expanded my thinking, helped me to take action in my own life, and gave me the information and ideas that I think will be helpful to everyone who uses this workbook.

How to Use This Book

This workbook is a practical, step-by-step guide for addressing, dealing with, and relieving the loneliness in your life. It is based on a study I conducted with over one-hundred people. I call it the *Loneliness Study*. Some of the Study respondents answered a questionnaire I wrote. Others attended focus groups I held or had personal interviews with me. The workbook also includes ideas I have gathered through years of work with people who experience various kinds of emotional distress. It is designed to help you explore the meaning of loneliness in your life by (1) considering the many options available to you to relieve loneliness; (2) implementing those options you wish to use; (3) increasing the number of connections you have with others; and (4) improving your old and new relationships.

It takes time and work to create the changes in your life that will improve your circumstances and make you feel better about yourself and your life. It is a lifelong process. I have been working on keeping a strong support system, finding companionship for myself, and dealing with my family and intimate relationships all my life. I know my experience is not unique. Although we all need and enjoy some time alone, there are very few of us who don't want and crave companionship and intimate relationships.

This book is organized by chapters. You may choose to spend more time on some chapters and less time on others. You may skip those chapters that don't seem to apply to you or that don't interest you. The chapters are arranged consecutively. Each chapter prepares you for the next one. You can, however, jump from chapter to chapter in any order you choose. This is a self-guided journey. There is no one right way to travel this road. Whatever steps you choose to take will be the right ones for you.

Work through this book slowly. It is not the kind of book that you sit down with and read in an evening or even in several sessions. You may want to read one short section, even a paragraph, do the exercises, think about them and work on the ideas, and then pick the book up again at another time to do another piece of this work.

Guidelines

1. You may have been lonely for a very long time. You may feel as if you will always be lonely. However, many people who have been lonely all of their lives do find ways to deal with it. They also find that, by relieving their loneliness so that it is only an occasional brief problem instead of an overwhelming issue, they significantly improve the overall quality of their lives.

2. You are always the person in charge. The readings, exercises, and activities are suggestions for how you can address issues related to loneliness in your life. It is always up to you to choose what you do. If doing something that is suggested doesn't feel right to you, then don't do it. This book is written with the hope that you will trust your intuition.

3. This is a workbook. It belongs to you personally. It was designed to be written in. One hurdle you often have to jump when you begin to use a workbook like this is to let go of the old rule that you must not write in books. Please write freely and easily in this book. Treat it like the kind of workbook you used in elementary or high school, the only difference being that there is no need to keep

it neat. No one is going to check your spelling or grammar, no one is going to grade your work, in fact, no one else is going to look at it unless *you* show it to them. The workbook itself and the thoughts you write in it are important tools for you to use to relieve your loneliness.

4. All of us learn in different ways—some of us through reading, others by hearing, feeling, writing, or doing. Some of us learn most easily when we are moving around, others when we are sitting quietly. Some of us like background music or noise when we are learning. Others prefer quiet. In this book there are choices about how to do many of the exercises and activities in order to respect different learning styles. Please reflect on your own learning style and try to support it throughout the book. In addition, feel free to use your creativity and adapt the exercises and activities to better match your learning style.

5. When doing this kind of work, structure is frequently helpful to many people. You might try setting aside an hour or so each week (more or less depending on what you want to do) to work on the readings, exercises, and activities. If this works for you, try doing it at the same time each day. Make a date with yourself and write it into your engagement calendar.

6. Don't try and do this work if you are very upset or feel very rushed. Wait until you feel better. Or do a relaxation exercise before beginning so you will be calm and be able to think clearly and effectively.

7. While you are doing this work, and always, take good care of yourself in every way. Eat well, exercise, spend time outdoors, and get plenty of rest. Spend as much time as possible with people you enjoy—people who make you feel good about yourself. Avoid people who don't treat you well. Do things that give you energy and peace, and don't forget the big and little things that give meaning to life.

8. Do not expect your loneliness to end quickly. You may have been dealing with it for a long time. As you work through this book and go on to use the things you have learned in your life, you will notice that you spend less time feeling lonely and more time feeling that you are closely connected to others. Giving yourself to others who give back to you in return creates an ever-increasing spiral of contentment.

CHAPTER 1

Exploring Loneliness

Loneliness is a feeling of having no common bond with the people around you. The feeling is akin to being an alien and all those around you are speaking of a language and life that you can see only in magazines. Loneliness is feeling disconnected and lost, even in the midst of family.

—Forty-two-year-old woman living with her husband and five small children.

When you find that you are uncomfortable with or don't like a particular situation, circumstance, or feeling in your life, and you want to create some change, a good first step is to "pull apart"—or "tease" apart—whatever it is you would like to change. In this chapter you will have the opportunity to "tease apart" your sense of loneliness. This means you will take a closer look at what being lonely means to you, what you feel and believe about loneliness, and how important it is to you to give some time and attention to relieving your feelings of loneliness. This process will provide clarity, confirm your feelings, and give you the motivation to begin working on this issue.

In chapter 2 you will take an inventory of your loneliness status and needs. That chapter will be followed by chapters that address the issues of enjoying time alone and self-esteem. These two factors seem to be key in determining how much loneliness someone experiences. Depression, discussed in chapter 15, "The Challenges of Loneliness," is often involved when people experience excessive loneliness, both as a cause and as a result of their loneliness.

Many years ago when I was an adolescent, an adult woman I knew described a dream she had had to me. She had dreamt about a great chasm—a chasm so deep that she couldn't see to its bottom—with steep rock cliffs on either side. She was alone on one side of the chasm, looking at the other side. On the other side people were talking to each other, laughing, and having a good time. There was no way for her to get to the other side where the people were—and she felt totally excluded and utterly alone.

Her dream has stayed with me throughout my life. There have been many times when I felt as if I were on one side of a chasm, looking across to a place where everyone else is having a good time. For me, this dream is a very clear description of loneliness.

A woman in the Loneliness Study said that when she is lonely, she imagines herself enveloped in a plastic bubble, just floating in space where no one can hear her and no one cares about her thoughts and feelings. She says that when she gets really lonely, she actually experiences a pain in her heart, as if there is a huge hole in it. It makes her feel like a lost soul, wondering if anyone would notice her absence if she were gone. Another woman said that loneliness means she is merely uncomfortable. She senses that her life could be richer, especially with regard to relationships, that there is the potential for more satisfying relationships.

One man described loneliness as feeling a gulf, an emptiness between his essential being and the world. He craves contact and intimacy as a means of confirming his existence on this earth—and it is somehow denied to him. Another man said, "Loneliness is like carrying around a vacuum chamber inside."

Now, in the space provided below, describe your personal images of loneliness.

Defining Loneliness

The American Heritage Dictionary of the English Language (1992) defines loneliness as: "the quality or state of being lonely." It then goes on to describe lonely as:

1. a. being without companions: lone; b. characterized by aloneness; solitary; 2. unfrequented by people: desolate, a lonely crossroad; 3. a. dejected by the awareness of being alone; b. producing such dejection: "the loneliest night of the week."

Do any of these definitions feel right to you? If they don't feel right, what's wrong with them?

Loneliness is always a unique experience. The word means different things to different people but, for most, a description of loneliness would include words that describe feelings. There is no one right way to define feelings of loneliness. You may describe them one way today and a totally different way at another time.

In the Loneliness Study, people wrote their own definitions of loneliness. These definitions contained many "feeling" words and phrases such as *despair, hopeless, emptiness, incompleteness, devoid of love,* and *longing for human contact.* A feeling is an emotional response to an event or circumstance. It can be brief, like the feeling of fear when you hear a loud noise, or long term, like the feelings of sadness and despair that you experience when a loved one is ill. A strong feeling creates a change in your normal state of being.

People in the Study defined loneliness with the following phrases: *without friends or a companion; feeling like you don't have anyone who wants to be with you; feeling abandoned and unable to connect with anyone on either a physical or emotional level; feeling left out; being alone and not comfortable with yourself; feeling as if there's nobody who cares about you; not having people around you when you want people around you,* and *missing people*.

What Does Loneliness Mean to You?

Let's explore what loneliness means to you. Read through the following exercise to make sure you understand what you will be doing. Then follow the directions.

Sit back in your chair. Make sure you feel comfortable. Take a few deep breaths. Now, focus your attention on the feeling of loneliness. To do this you may need to think of a time in your life when you were lonely. If there are physical sensations that go along with the feeling, focus your attention on them. Pay attention to all of your feelings. Stay with them. Hold them in your mind for a few minutes. Take your time. Try to focus on these feelings for several minutes.

Now, describe what you felt during the exercise? Write freely. Describe anything that comes into your mind.

_____

_____

_____

Hopefully, you've now got some insight into what your personal experience of loneliness is like. Keep this insight in mind, and let's think about the opposite of loneliness for a while. To overcome loneliness we need to define what it is we'd rather be feeling.

What Would It Feel Like If You Were *Not* Lonely?

Just as you have times when you feel lonely, you also have times when you don't feel lonely. One man in the Study said, "When I am not lonely, I feel connected to the people I am with. I feel like they understand and respect me and that we are all enjoying this time that we are sharing."

One key word related to *not* feeling lonely is *balance*—a balance between being with others and being alone. Some other words and phrases that people in the Loneliness Study used to describe *not* being lonely were *connection with others; sharing a common bond or experience; feeling loved; connection such that even when you are by yourself you feel bonded to someone; that others are there and will be there in spirit if not in person for you always.* Others said that: *it's feeling like you have true friends and close family; the security of having someone there for you when you need them; togetherness; when your mind is full of ideas and not focused on being lonely; feeling whole/complete, loved, and a sense of belonging; a sense of community and being fully engaged with others.*

Which of the previous words and phrases describe how you feel, have felt, or would like to feel if you were not lonely? What other words and phrases and images come to you? Write them in below.

_____

_____

_____

Once again, let's do an exploratory exercise. Sit back in your chair. Make sure you feel comfortable. Take a few deep breaths. Focus on feeling *not* lonely. To do this, you may need to think of a time in your life when you were not lonely. If you can't think of such a time, imagine such a time. Take your time. Focus on these feelings for several minutes. Enjoy these good feelings. Luxuriate in them.

Now, describe below how you felt during this exercise.

_____

_____

_____

Keep in mind whatever insights may have come to you, and let's go on.

Is Loneliness Always Bad?

Some people feel that, from time to time, loneliness is okay. In responding to the Study one woman said, "I just realized that in all these questions, there is the assumption that loneliness is 'bad,' something to be gotten rid of. I'm not sure I agree with that premise. I think if we can 'hang out' with loneliness, we can learn a lot about ourselves and the world." A man in the Study said, "Loneliness isn't life or death. I can go to a movie alone, or just feel bad for a while."

Another man in the Study said, "Sometimes loneliness has been the catalyst for self-reflection—periods of time that have helped me to reassess what I believe, what I think is important. Loneliness is not such a bad thing, in my opinion. Sometimes it's nice to feel empty. Then our hearts can be open for other things to fill us up. If we're always completely satisfied, filled, or whatever, perhaps we would become stagnated."

How do you feel about this? Are there any times when loneliness feels tolerable to you or times when you believe that some loneliness is acceptable? If so, when do you feel all right about being lonely?

_____

_____

_____

If you need more space to write your answer than is provided, just insert a sheet of paper into the book here. Or keep a separate journal while you read to record all of your responses and impressions. Go as far into this exploration as you feel drawn to do. Allow yourself to learn more about the richness and complexity of your own unique self. When you're done, let's go on to the next topic.

Being Lonely and Being Alone

People in the Loneliness Study agreed that feeling lonely and being alone are very different. For example, one woman said that when she is alone she often doesn't feel lonely at all. She feels that her most intense lonely feelings derive from being "invisible" to those around her, and from the emptiness that comes from her beliefs that she has no inner resources to draw upon, and nothing of value to give to others. To her, isolation is the result of pulling back from others because of fear or other negative beliefs about herself.

One man in the Study said that he was able to be alone and still be very happy because he doesn't feel lonely if he is doing something he considers useful, productive, and has a sense of accomplishment. He said he can be alone as long as he feels as if he is making a difference in his life or someone else's. However, he also said that when he is lonely, it is very painful for him because he feels as if he is cut off from the rest of the world—especially when he doesn't feel as if he even belongs in his own house with his own family.

One woman said that being alone can be either very pleasant—or not, but that loneliness hurts. She said that loneliness always desires contact. A man said that feeling lonely is always combined with sadness, while being alone is not necessarily sad.

Do you feel there is a difference between loneliness and being alone? If so, describe that difference.

_____

_____

_____

You can increase your understanding of your feelings of loneliness by doing the following exercises:

1. Remember and describe ten examples of the times in your life when you felt really lonely.

2. Remember and describe ten times in your life when you did *not* feel lonely.

3. Ask several friends or family members what loneliness feels like to them, and have them describe for you the times in their lives when they felt lonely and the times when they did *not* feel lonely. Insert your writing into the workbook here if you like.

CHAPTER 2

Loneliness in Your Life

For me, loneliness doesn't become a problem until it is starting to affect the way I feel. When I realize I am getting a hard feeling in the pit of my stomach, I know I need to reach out to others.

—Fifty-five-year-old woman living alone

You have now given some attention to defining loneliness. Before you begin looking at specific ways to relieve loneliness in your life, you need to think about the loneliness in *your* life and what it is you really want. This chapter will help you to do that. It will also help you to identify and address some negative thought patterns that may be causing your loneliness or keeping you from reaching out to others.

How to Determine When Loneliness Is a Problem

One important factor in understanding your own loneliness is knowing where you fall in the range that varies from "loner" to "people person." Everyone differs in how much connection they want with other people. Some people like to be around other people all the time. Others find that occasional social contact is satisfactory. When people don't have as much contact and connection with others as they would like, loneliness becomes an issue. Some people in the study reported that they feel lonely even when they are with others—family members, friends, or in a crowd of strangers.

Some people never think much about loneliness at all. People come and go in their life. Sometimes they miss people when they leave and wish for closer connection with others, but it's never a big problem for them. They don't need to do any planning or take any action to relieve loneliness. Other people feel as if they have always been lonely. When loneliness is a problem for you that has recurred over and over again, and you want to do something about it, it will take some attention, planning, and action to re-create your life the way you want it to be.

Some people in the study considered loneliness a problem when their lives were not filled with meaningful or purposeful activity, and they had little to look forward to. Others related it to feelings of hurting beyond the normal level of sadness, or when they felt isolated even when interacting with friends and acquaintances. Some people said that feelings of loneliness become a problem when they interfere with personal relationships.

At these times, people noted they don't feel heard or understood; they feel very different and separate from others and lose the capacity to feel intimacy with another.

Many people said loneliness becomes a problem for them when it affects their self-worth and feelings of being loved or lovable. They mentioned feelings of shutting down, and the desire to avoid others and avoid talking about feelings. Others said loneliness is a problem for them when it causes deep, inescapable feelings of sadness, sometimes accompanied by bouts of crying.

Still others felt loneliness becomes a problem when they stop answering the phone or the doorbell, stay at home, and go out of their way to avoid people whom they usually like to interact with. Some of these people said the length of time these feelings persisted was an indicator for them of loneliness issues that need to be addressed.

When does loneliness become a problem for you—a problem that you want to address?

_____

_____

_____

What Does Being "Less Lonely" Mean to You?

The following list describes what feeling less lonely means to other people. When you think of being less lonely, what does that mean to you? Check only the responses that are important to you.

Does being less lonely mean:

_____ enjoying spending time by myself

_____ feeling as if I am really "with" others when we are together

_____ having my loneliness relieved by being with others

_____ having an intimate relationship

_____ having several close friends

_____ having people I can talk to when I am having a hard time

_____ having people I can check in with on a regular basis

_____ having people call me for support when they are having a hard time

_____ getting more mail

_____ having connections with others via the Internet

_____ living where there are lots of other people to talk to all the time

_____ joining a support group

_____ being an active member of a support group

_____ traveling with others

_____ going to more community activities like concerts and movies

_____ volunteering

_____ having friends or having more friends

_____ inviting friends to come to my home or to visit their homes more often

_____ having gatherings in my home

_____ being invited to get together with others or get together with others more often

What else does being less lonely mean to you?

_____

_____

_____

Insert more pages or write further in your separate journal and really explore this idea as much as you can. The more you focus on what it is you want, the easier it will be to see what steps you must take to get what you want.

How Many Close Friends or Supporters Would You Like?

You are the only person who can decide how you want your life to be and what you want to do about your loneliness. In our society, institutions such as schools and churches, and people such as health care professionals and even family members and friends may believe that they have the right to determine the course of someone else's life. But this is not true. We each have the right to shape our lives the way we want to, so long as we do not infringe on anyone else's rights. You will not be satisfied with the results of your work on loneliness if someone else is "steering your ship."

As you proceed with this work you will be thinking about your life, making some plans, and making some decisions. Remember, a decision is never "set in stone." It can always be changed. My mother used to say, "If you haven't changed your mind lately, maybe you don't have one." What you choose as a goal or an action to take this week may change as you proceed with this workbook and learn more about yourself, your life, and what feels right to you.

One goal for alleviating loneliness that has worked well for many people is to have five supporters—they might be family members, friends, or coworkers—so that there would always be someone available when you would like:

someone to talk to • companionship • help in figuring things out and decision making • to have a good time

If you only have one friend or supporter, and that person becomes ill, goes away on vacation, or is busy at work, and you would like some companionship, no one will be available. If there was something upsetting going on in your life such as an impending divorce, a sick child, or the loss of your job, with only one friend there might be no one available to support you. So it is advisable to have more than one close person in your life. Nevertheless, it is still your choice.

You may want many more people in your life than five—or you may want fewer. How many friends or supporters do you think you would like? Why do you think that number of friends or supporters would work well for you?

_____

_____

How Do You See Your Friends and Supporters Involved in Your Life?

Do you have an intimate, satisfying physical relationship with another person? If not, would you like to have such a person in your life? If you don't have an intimate, satisfying relationship with another person, and would like to have such a relationship, how do you think it would help you to relieve loneliness?

_____

_____

_____

Do you have close family members who meet some of your needs some of the time and keep you from being lonely at other times? Explain:

_____

_____

_____

Do you sometimes wish you could create a new family for yourself? If so, what would your new family be like? Describe:

_____

_____

_____

The answers you have written to these questions convey important information about yourself that you need to keep clearly in mind. Look back frequently to these writings as you work through this workbook and feel free to change your answers as you grow and learn. What you write about yourself during such explorations can become important "touchstones."

What Attributes Do You Want Your Friends and Supporters to Have?

Each of us wants different things from our friends. While I like friends who can go hiking with me and who are interested in environmental issues, these activities and concerns may not be important to you at all.

One friend may play a certain role in your life while another may play an entirely different one. For instance, when you want someone to go for a long walk with you, you might call Susan, but when you need a really good listener to share a personal problem you are having, Susan might not be suitable, but Sarah or Bruce would be a good choice.

Which of the following characteristics do you want your friends to have? If it is very important, give it three checks, if it is somewhat important give it two checks. If it would just be all right, give it one check. If it is not what you want at all, don't check it.

I want friends and supporters who:

_____ care about me

_____ empathize with me

_____ affirm and validate me and my experience

_____ ignore my disability and treat me the same as anyone else

_____ accept me as I am even when I'm in a bad mood

_____ don't try to change me

_____ don't stand me up when we have appointments

_____ don't have me "all figured out"

_____ don't pry into my past

_____ don't mind spending time with my small children

_____ listen to me

_____ share their lives with me

_____ like to cook a meal together from time to time

_____ advocate for me

_____ enjoy sharing fun and interesting activities with me

_____ are willing to work with me to resolve conflicts

_____ make me laugh about my troubles

_____ avoid judging me, criticizing me, "putting me down," or teasing me

_____ love me unconditionally

_____ set me straight when I'm getting myself into trouble

_____ remind me to be patient with myself

What other attributes would you like your friends or supporters to have? Again, use the checking system used above to determine how important these attributes are to you.

_____

_____

_____

Assets That You Bring to a Friendship

You have some very special qualities that you can bring to friendships and supportive relationships. For instance, you may be a very patient person and be very understanding of people with certain disabilities. You may be able to speak several languages. You may enjoy having intellectual and political discussions. Or you may really enjoy supporting people who are trying to start a career. Although this may feel like a difficult task—for many people it does—take a close look at yourself, and make a list of the special qualities or assets that you bring to relationships with others. The ideas on what you would like to receive from your friends and supporters in the previous section will help you to assess your own special attributes and to know what you will bring to relationships in return.

_____

_____

_____

Identifying Supporters in Your Life Now

Although no one person can meet all of your needs for companionship and support, do you have some people in your life who meet many of these needs? If so, who are they and which of the characteristics that you checked above do these friends best meet?

Person   **Attributes**

_____   _____

_____   _____

_____   _____

These people are very important. Try to think of at least one person you can put on this list now. Maybe it is a health care professional, a coworker, or a family member. The work you are doing by reading this book, answering these questions, and taking action based on what you learn will help you find more people you can put on this list.

An Ideal Scenario

Vast differences came up when people in the study were asked to identify an ideal scenario for themselves—one in which they would not feel lonely. For instance, some people said it would include many people while others said there would be only a few or even only one person. One person said that being in large groups is just too stressful for her. Some said that sometimes they like to be with large groups of people where little intimacy is shared while at other times they like to be with just one or several people where they can connect with each other on a deeper level. Some people said that when they are with larger groups of people they enjoy playing host or hostess, that is, orchestrating the group to some extent.

Now, take a few deep breaths. Using the information you have learned about yourself in this chapter, imagine yourself in a situation with others where you feel really comfortable and supported—not lonely. Take a few minutes to design this situation in your mind. Don't try to do it quickly. When you feel that you have established an ideal set of circumstances in your mind, describe that situation.

_____

_____

_____

Did your ideal situation include some people you already know? If so, who were they and what is it about them that makes you feel comfortable?

Person's name: _____

Describe why you feel good when you are with this person:

_____

_____

_____

Person's name: _____

Describe why you feel good when you are with this person:

_____

_____

Person's name: _____

Describe why you feel good when you are with this person:

_____

_____

_____

Setting Goals

Review the information you have covered in this chapter. Based on what you have discovered about your own needs and assets, what do you think you would like to achieve to relieve your loneliness. Don't worry about how you are going to achieve these goals yet, just write down what you would really like for yourself regarding connection with others (remember, you can come back to these goals at any time and revise or change them):

In one month

_____

_____

In six months

_____

_____

In one year

_____

_____

In five years

_____

_____

Change Negative Thoughts About Loneliness to Positive Ones

When you were a child, you may have learned to think negatively about loneliness in ways that continue to affect you and the way you do things in your life today. Such thoughts may have kept you from feeling good about yourself and from getting into meaningful relationships with others. Everyone has some ideas that they accept as "truths" until they examine those ideas more closely. Upon closer scrutiny, you may discover that some of your ideas about loneliness are untrue.

When you become aware of ideas that you believe are true without ever having questioned them because they were absorbed when you were very young, or because the source seemed valid, it is often helpful to first examine such ideas and then try to loosen the hold they have over your life. Following are some of the most common negative thought patterns that affect loneliness. There is also a suggestion for a more positive thought you might use to replace the negative thought.

Some of the ideas you have may be distorted thought patterns that cause you to feel lonely or increase your loneliness. You may also discover other negative thought patterns that you want to change.

Negative thought: If I had been popular in high school, I would never be lonely.

Another way to look at this: Being popular in high school does not keep you from being lonely later in your life.

What do *you* believe is the best way to look at this?

_____

_____

Negative thought: Other people can fill the "empty spaces" I have in myself. Other people can make me feel lovable.

Another way to look at this: *You* have to fill the "empty spaces" inside of yourself. Others cannot do that for you. It is important to love yourself and feel loved by others.

What do *you* believe is the best way to look at this?

_____

_____

Negative thought: If I was thin, or smart, or beautiful, or rich, or famous . . . I wouldn't be lonely.

Another way to look at this: These kinds of qualities may have some effect on loneliness but, in blaming your loneliness on them, you miss out on opportunities to make strong connections with other people. Being compassionate and supportive of others is more likely to alleviate loneliness than being thin, smart, rich, beautiful, or famous.

What do *you* believe is the best way to look at this?

_____

_____

Negative thought: Once I have some good friends or an intimate relationship, I will never be lonely again.

Another way to look at this: Everyone feels lonely from time to time.

What do *you* believe is the best way to look at this?

_____

_____

Negative thought: If you have been rejected once, you always will be rejected.

Another way to look at this: If you were rejected once, it means only that. It doesn't mean you always will be rejected.

What do *you* believe is the best way to look at this?

_____

_____

Negative thought: Anything that goes wrong in a relationship is my fault.

Another way to look at this: Both people in a relationship can do things that create difficulties.

What do *you* believe is the best way to look at this?

_____

_____

Negative thought: If this relationship doesn't work out, it means I am a total failure.

Another way to look at this: If this relationship doesn't work out, it only means that the relationship didn't work out. It does not mean you are a failure.

What do *you* believe is the best way to look at this?

_____

_____

Negative thought: I can tell what others are feeling even though they haven't said anything.

Another way to look at this: It is not a good idea to assume that you know what others are feeling. If you want to know how they are feeling, ask them.

What do *you* believe is the best way to look at this?

_____

_____

Negative thought: There is really something wrong with me because none of my relationships ever work out.

Another way to look at this: There are many different reasons why relationships don't work out. The fact that my relationships have not worked out does not mean something is wrong with me.

What do *you* believe is the best way to look at this?

_____

_____

As you reviewed these negative thoughts, you may have realized that you have some other negative thoughts or ideas about loneliness and being connected with others that are making you more lonely or that are keeping you from being able to relieve your loneliness. For instance, a twenty-year-old woman in the Loneliness Study thought that her friends had to be the same age as she is and come from a similar educational background. When she realized that she could have friends of any age, and that differences in educational background do not necessarily have anything to do with whether a person might be a good friend, she made some strong connections with others that have greatly helped to relieve her loneliness.

Use the following spaces to write down any of your negative thoughts about loneliness and connection with others, along with positive statements you can use to change these negative thoughts to positive ones.

1. Negative thought about loneliness

_____

_____

How does having this negative thought benefit me?

_____

_____

How does having this negative thought keep me from taking positive action to relieve my loneliness?

_____

_____

Do you want to change this negative thought to a positive one? If you do want to change this negative thought to a positive one, write a positive statement that replaces your negative thought that feels right to you. (See the question "What do *you* believe is the best way to look at this?" in the previous exercise and think about your answers.)

2. Negative thought about loneliness

_____

How does having this negative thought benefit me?

How does having this negative thought keep me from taking positive action to relieve my loneliness?

Do you want to change this negative thought to a positive one? If you want to change this negative thought to a positive one, write a positive statement that contradicts your negative thought that feels right to you. (See the question "What do *you* believe is the best way to look at this?" in the previous exercise.)

After you have decided on a positive thought to replace your negative thought, you need to reinforce it over and over again until you automatically think the positive thought instead of the negative one. You do this by replacing the negative thought with the positive one every time you "catch" yourself thinking the negative thought. The way to replace a negative habitual thought with an habitual positive one is to write it over and over again in your journal; say it to yourself over and over again; and/or write the positive thoughts on Post-it "stickies" and place them in prominent places around your house so you will read them frequently.

CHAPTER 3

Relieving Loneliness

In general I have consistent, supportive, effective ways to deal with the loneliness that arises out of various life situations. These methods are not intentions to rid myself of loneliness but rather to explore, and prevent myself from slipping into the cycle of despair and depression. I expect to feel lonely at times. The depth of it is what I notice and attempt to make a bit more shallow and manageable.

—Single man in his late thirties

Everyone has lonely times. The loneliness may last for a few hours, a few days, a few months—or you may feel as if you have always been lonely. This chapter will focus on specific techniques that can be used to relieve loneliness in the short term. These techniques can be used if you are having a lonely afternoon, day, or series of days. Some of them, if used consistently, may relieve long-term loneliness. They can be used consistently on a long-term basis.

There is no one right answer for everyone on how to relieve loneliness at any given time. No one else can tell you what will relieve *your* loneliness. You need to figure this out for yourself—and much of the figuring out you do will be through trying out different techniques to see what feels best and works well for you. As you read about the methods described this chapter, think about which ones feel right to you—and decide which you would like to try. If you aren't sure, try them anyway—if it feels right, you can keep doing it, if it doesn't, you can stop.

As you read through these ideas, you will probably think of ways to relieve your loneliness that aren't mentioned here. This chapter also includes information on unsuccessful strategies that people have used to relieve loneliness.

Simple Ideas for Quickly Relieving Loneliness

Read through the following list of ideas for quickly and simply relieving loneliness—the kind of loneliness you may feel on a quiet afternoon when everyone in your household is away, or when your closest friend is on vacation. Used one time, they will probably help you feel better. However, if you use them consistently for longer periods of time, they might help you deal with deeper issues of loneliness, such as the lonely times you experienced when you were a child.

- **Recognize the feeling of loneliness and make a clear decision to "be with" those feelings.** In the Loneliness Study, people referred to this as "acceptance" or "riding it out." Reminding yourself that loneliness passes can be helpful to this process. (This is not a good idea if you feel as if you have always been lonely.) One woman said, "I just realized the assumption is that loneliness is 'bad,' something to be gotten rid of. I'm not sure I agree with that premise. It's the same way people feel that boredom is bad and to be gotten rid of, whereas I suspect that if we can learn to hang out with boredom, we learn a lot about ourselves and our world. I think the same may be true of loneliness."

- **Fake cheerfulness.** Play act cheerfulness until you really feel it. You might sing, dance to the radio or a favorite CD, watch a funny video, recall jokes you enjoyed in the past or a very humorous incident in your life, practice laughing aloud to yourself, or read a book of cartoons.

- **Meditate.** Redirect your mind to concentrate on positive, inner-directed energies by sitting quietly and focusing your attention on your breathing, or on some object such as a candle flame, or a self-affirming thought. This might include prayer or connecting with your spiritual resources.

- **Divert your attention away from loneliness to other matters**. Think about the good time you had last week, an outing you have planned, or an anticipated positive change in your life. See chapter 4, "Enjoying Time Alone"; there are many ideas there for diverting your attention from loneliness.

- **Keep busy.** One man in the Study said, "When I was eighteen and nineteen years old I was attending junior college in a new city and made no close friends; perhaps I was lonely but maybe not. To fill my time and to prevent loneliness I went to school, worked to save money for a European trip, and spent as much time as I could at the beach (this was in southern California). If I hadn't been so busy—maybe I would have been lonely."

- **Release your emotions**. Have a good cry or pound on a pillow. Be sure to be in a place that feels really comfortable, comforting, and safe to you when you do this.

- **Call a friend.** Have a long, satisfying, two-way conversation. Let your hair down and talk about everything you have been thinking about.

- **Ask someone to join you for a while**. Meet for lunch, a walk, a movie, or some other activity.

- **Talk to people wherever you are**. Engage in small talk wherever you happen to be—rest rooms, supermarket lines, on the bus, etc.

- **Spend some time in a local cafe or coffee shop**. Pick one that is friendly, and read the newspaper or a book you have brought along. Sometimes just being in a public space with other people present helps to relieve loneliness.

- **Help others**. Do something nice for someone else. One woman in the Study said that she gives out five compliments every day to those people with whom she interacts. It may be telling a checkout girl you appreciate her speed, telling a coworker she or he has done a great job, telling your partner what a fantastic person he or she is, or telling your child how much you like the way he or she smiles or helps out around the house.

- **Communicate with someone**. Write a letter, send a card, or send an email.

- **Communicate with yourself**. Write in your journal.

- **Do something that needs to be done**. Take care of a long-deferred task and then luxuriate in the feeling of having completed it.

- **Exercise.** Physical exertion of any kind—be it stretching, working out with small weights, riding a stationary bike in your bedroom, or jogging outdoors—will make you feel better physically and alleviate loneliness.

- **Give yourself a massage**. You can give yourself a gentle massage by softly rubbing all the parts of your body. Concentrate on those parts that ache or are stiff.

- **Eat something**. Prepare and eat a delicious comfort food. (This is not suggested if overeating, undereating, or food are difficult issues for you.)

- **Play a musical instrument**. If you don't own an instrument, buy a small hand drum. Drumming on a small hand drum is especially good because you can do it without needing to take lessons. Or buy a pennywhistle or a harmonica and try to play some simple tunes.

- **Sing aloud**. Sing along with your favorite radio program or an old beloved record or CD. Or sing aloud by yourself. Try to remember the words of songs you loved when you were a child.

- **Read.** Read an enjoyable novel for pleasure or read something that is hard to understand but interests you. Take notes. You may find that if you really focus on it, it will begin to seem less difficult.

- **Do something creative**. Draw or paint a picture. Make a photo collage. Knit or crochet something. Do some wood carving or wax modeling. Compose a song or write a poem.

- **Play with your pet**. (See the section on pets later in this chapter.) One person in the Study said, "My dog is a friend I can always count on."

- **Check in with your friends on the Internet.** (See the section on the Internet later in this chapter.)
- **Try to enjoy your time alone**. Give yourself a break from looking for people to be your friends and focus your attention on raising your self-esteem and enjoying your time alone. See chapter 4, "Enjoying Time Alone," and chapter 5, "The Self Esteem/Loneliness Connection."

Now, list any other ways you have used successfully to relieve loneliness.

_____

_____

You might make a list of the activities you find most useful for relieving short-term loneliness and post that list in a convenient place so you will see it when you are lonely. It can serve as a useful reminder that there are steps you can take to combat loneliness.

Pets

One man in the Loneliness Study said, "When I have been lonely in my life, my dog has always been there for me. He's always home. He's never 'too busy.' He loves me and accepts me unconditionally, even when I'm in a bad mood." A woman said, "I would never be without a cat. If I didn't have a cat, I am afraid the loneliness would overtake me." Dogs and cats were the most popular pets mentioned by those in the Study. However, some people reported that birds and even fish were very important to them and helped them relieve their loneliness. Some found that association even with farm animals like horses, goats, and cows also helped them to relieve their loneliness.

For all of their wonderful attributes, it's not always easy or possible to have a pet. Having a pet requires a consistent commitment. Pet food and veterinary care can be expensive and pets must be fed and cared for. There are regulations in many communities about where pets can go and how they must be managed. Many rental units and condominiums do not allow pets or large pets.

Using the Internet to Relieve Loneliness

A woman in the Study said, "I use the computer daily to combat loneliness. Without it, I would be in deep despair. Basically, it helps me to get outside of myself. Some days it allows me to pursue my interests, do research, and plan workshops. It helps me to find articles that interest me and others; it informs me about people I have heard about but don't really know; it helps me to plan travel; it provides me with information to share with others, and much more. I think I could easily slip into despair without it. With it I can talk with people, go to other worlds, find others, and find books. It expands my world."

A person in the Loneliness Study said, "I use the Internet to combat loneliness. I have found the chat rooms helpful when I needed to talk to someone and did not feel there was anyone whom I could lean on. There are numerous sites that deal with psychology and depression and other emotions. Many of them offer chat rooms where one can share with others what they are feeling." Another person in the Study said, "To the extent that loneliness is relieved simply by filling the space, I think the Internet helps a lot. For me, it is mostly just tantalizing. It doesn't take the place of being with people." Another man said, "Chat rooms make it possible to talk to people about anything, somewhat anonymously. And it does make the time fly!" One woman reported that she had Internet pen pals in India, Texas, Arizona, and Russia and finds this to be the best way for her to have friends. Another woman said, "I make friends online that I never have met and never plan to meet, so that if I pour my heart out to them I don't fear ridicule."

One woman said the Internet was not helpful to her. She said it encouraged her antisocial behavior. Still another woman in the Study said, "I tried AOL's chat rooms for a brief period but was disappointed by the superficial interactions on line. I felt even lonelier after experiencing that."

There are many reasons for and against using the Internet to relieve loneliness. If it is used along with other techniques for relieving loneliness, the Internet can be a powerful tool for connecting with others, in addition to being a wonderful source on information on virtually any topic. Although it does not allow face-to-face connection, it does gives you the opportunity to communicate with others through newsgroups, message boards, chat rooms, and email lists.

When using the Internet you can be anonymous and can talk about real and sensitive issues without revealing your identity. It gives you quick access to others who know and understand what you are talking about. You not only receive support for yourself, but you also can feel good about giving support to someone else. For one monthly fee (if that service is available in your area) you can talk to anyone around the world.

One woman had this to say about email: "Email is great as it provides the intensity of interaction with the immediacy of response that can be essential. Belonging to lists is good, sometimes. It also allows you to search for organizations that interest you, within which low-risk interaction can occur, for example, posting a message, accessing meetings, and so forth."

The following brief descriptions of each Internet communication option will give you some idea of what to expect. If you need more information on using the Internet to find companionship and support, contact the National Mental Health Consumers Self-Help Clearinghouse at http://www.mhselfhelp.org or by email at info@mhselfhelp.org and ask them for their technical assistance guide, *Advocacy and Recovery Using the Internet*.

Newsgroups. Newsgroups are great places to ask questions and share information and experience. People write in questions or pieces of information. These are called postings. Others in the newsgroup can post a response. You can find newsgroups that address just about any topic through http://www.deja.com or http://listz.com.

Message Boards or Bulletin Boards. These are very similar to newsgroups, but not as busy. The advantage—or you may see this as a disadvantage—is that someone maintains the board so you will not receive any inappropriate postings, such as advertisements or personal attacks. You can find links to these boards at various Web sites. You might try http://www.support-group.com/support.htm.

Chat Rooms: The chat room is most like talking directly to other people. Many chat rooms are focused on specific topics. However, you can talk about anything you want to talk about. Some are friendlier than others. You will want to check out several of these to find the one that feels best to you. To participate in a chat room, you must be online at the same time as the other person is online. To be sure you will find someone, you may want to participate in scheduled chat rooms. To find chat rooms where you can discuss personal and emotional issues, you can go to a search engine such as Yahoo or Excite and type in "mental health chat." For a scheduled "chat" you could check out http://www.support-group.com or http://www.drkoop.com.

Email Lists: You can subscribe to email lists that automatically send messages to you via email. You can even do this through a computer at your library by getting a free email address at http://www.hotmail.com. Some lists have restrictions on who can access them, others allow only those messages that are approved by the list manager, and some allow you to join and send messages to the group. The advantage of these lists is you receive messages without having to look for them. The disadvantage is if you join too many lists, you receive more mail than you will ever get a chance to read. You can find a catalogue of lists at http://www.listz.com and http://www.onlist.com.

In addition to finding supportive people on the Internet, you can use it to have fun by searching for topics that interest you. Although the cost of computers may have kept you from purchasing one in the past, computer prices continue to drop. Keep track of their prices so that you can purchase one when it becomes affordable for you. There are also special inexpensive models designed only for email and Internet capability. Another option is a less expensive rebuilt model. Also, access to email is expected to soon become available through cable TV.

If you have not used the Internet as a way to relieve loneliness, why not think about trying it?

Unsuccessful Methods for Relieving Loneliness
Sometimes loneliness can become so overwhelming that you try strategies that have an adverse affect on your life. For example, trying to relieve loneliness may put you in contact with people who treat you badly. Other strategies are not recommended because they don't work or they don't work well. Review the following list and see how you feel. Be sure to check off any strategies that you want to avoid.

- Avoiding addressing issues related to depression

- Clinging to a particular person or people

- Watching lots of television

- Spending most of your time on the Internet

- Drinking alcohol, smoking pot, overeating, workaholism, or any other addictive behavior

- "Hanging out" in bars or in unsafe areas of the community

- Isolating yourself for long periods of time with an object, idea, or activity such as reading, or a special project as a way to avoid being with people

- Avoiding spending time with others for fear of rejection

- Trying to keep yourself *very* busy

- Spending time with people who treat you badly

- Getting intensively involved in a cause you don't really believe in just for the company
- Joining a group or community that takes over control of your life

List other efforts to relieve loneliness you may have tried that were *not* helpful or that you think would not be helpful to you.

Letting Go of Loneliness

A woman in the Loneliness Study shared this meditation exercise for "letting go" of loneliness. It is a Buddhist technique for working with the mind called *tonglen*. Sit or lie down in a quiet space. Focus your attention on your breathing. As you breathe in, take in all the things that you would usually push away. In this case, you would take in loneliness, abandonment, inability to connect or communicate—all the aspects of this subject that you most want to get rid of—and then as you breathe out, you breathe out whatever you most want, in this case, friendship, connectedness, relaxation, confidence, whatever. This exercise can have the effect of shifting our usual way of being in the world altogether.

Next Steps

As I researched loneliness, it became clear to me that people who enjoy spending time alone and who feel good about themselves (have high self-esteem) experience less loneliness than people who don't like being alone and who don't like and value themselves. If either of these issues are problems for you, you may find some helpful solutions in the next two chapters.

CHAPTER 4

Enjoying Time Alone

My time alone is precious to me. I must have some of it every day to get in touch with myself—who I am and what I want.

—Forty-year-old single man

In reviewing the results of the Loneliness Study, it became clear that those people who enjoy spending time alone feel lonely less often, and that when they are lonely it is not "as deep" a feeling as it is for those who said they do not like to spend time alone. Therefore, learning to enjoy spending time alone is important to relieving loneliness in your life.

Everyone spends time alone. Most people prefer to have a balance between the time they spend alone and the time they spend with others. One woman in the study said she likes being alone so much it keeps her from being with others. Others spoke of "being happy with their own company."

It is not possible to be with someone all the time. However, some people feel lonely whenever they are alone or most of the time when they are alone. They may fear being alone and have a hard time feeling happy and secure when they are alone. They may even feel very anxious when they are alone. If you feel this way, it can become a serious issue in your life. Sometimes, one of the real dangers of not wanting to be alone is that, in desperation, you may find yourself spending time with people who treat you badly. You also may become dependent on others. You may find yourself always trying to arrange for someone to be with you. Other people may tire of this and back away. A more successful strategy is to learn to enjoy spending time alone. If you need to work on this, this chapter will give you some ideas on what to do.

If you already enjoy time alone, you may feel that you don't need to do the work on this topic. But try scanning the chapter. You may find some ideas that will help your time alone become even richer.

Why You Might Not Like Spending Time Alone

A good way to begin learning to enjoy your time alone is to consider the reasons why you don't like being alone and then to explore some options for creating change. Check off those ideas that you think would be helpful to you.

1. You feel unsafe—that there is no one to protect you.
   To counteract this try the following suggestions:

   Repeat affirmations like the ones below over and over.

   > *I am safe.*
   > *I can take care of myself.*

   Now, list some other affirmations you can think of that might help:

   _____

   _____

   Sing to yourself.

   Play music or the radio to divert your attention.

   Take some deep breaths—then divert your attention by doing something you enjoy. (There are ideas for things to do later in this chapter.)

   Now, list some other ways that you can think of to counteract your fear of being alone.

   _____

   _____

   _____

2. You feel that your living space is not safe from intruders.
   To counteract this you could do the following:

   Check windows and doors to make sure they are locked.

   Make sure your home is as safe from intrusion as possible by having adequate locks and barriers (you may need help from a landlord to make this happen).

   Move to a safer neighborhood.

   Now, list some other ways that you can think of to counteract your fear of being alone.

   _____

   _____

3. Being alone makes you feel that you are unloved—that no one ever wants to be with you.
To counteract this you could do the following:

Say STOP to yourself every time you notice that you are thinking or saying to yourself that being alone means you are unloved. Then repeat over and over, "Being alone does not mean I am unloved."

Now, make a list of the people who love you, even when they are not with you.

_____

_____

_____

List some other ways to counteract your sense of feeling unloved.

_____

_____

4. You don't like focusing on yourself. Some people are very uncomfortable being with themselves. You may not like "looking" too closely at yourself. When others are around, your attention is diverted and you don't have to focus on yourself. However, your life would be more enjoyable if you could enjoy being with yourself—if you didn't have to distract yourself from yourself by always being around other people.
To counteract this you could do the following:

Work on the activities listed above, as well as the other activities in this chapter. These activities are designed to help you like yourself and to feel comfortable with yourself. Also refer to chapter 5, "The Self-Esteem/Loneliness Connection."

Now, list some other reasons you think you don't like being alone. Then write some creative actions you could take to change that thought and the feelings connected to that thought.

I don't like being alone because

_____

Actions I could take to change that:

_____

_____

I don't like being alone because

_____

Actions I could take to change that:

_____

_____

Building on Your Interests and Special Abilities

Everyone has strengths that they can use to create change in their life—change like learning to enjoy time spent alone. For instance, one person in the study said she uses "alone time" to develop her musical abilities. Another woman said she uses time alone to develop a deeper and richer spiritual life. One man listens to tapes to learn foreign languages. So far, he has learned three. His new linguistic skills eventually resulted in a new career for him. People who have a wide range of interests they enjoy pursuing alone find this to be a great asset. They say it helps them through difficult times when they might otherwise be very lonely—like after retiring from a hectic professional life, or following the loss of a loved one.

The following activities will help you discover the interests and special abilities you have that will help you learn how to enjoy the time that you spend alone.

Describe a time when you were alone that you enjoyed.

_____

_____

List three things about that time that made it special for you.

1. _____

2. _____

3. _____

How could you arrange to have more times like that in your life?

_____

_____

Are you going to do it? ____ y ____ n
Why or why not?

_____

_____

Describe another time when you enjoyed the time that you spent alone.

_____

_____

List three things about that time that made it special for you.

1. _____

2. _____

3. _____

How could you arrange to have more times like that in your life?

_____

_____

Are you going to do it? ____ y ____ n
Why or why not?

_____

If you think it would be helpful, you can repeat this exercise again and again to help you determine how you can make your time alone more pleasant.

Taking a Look Back

Looking at activities that you enjoyed at other times in your life, even when you were a child, may help you discover some things you could do that would make your time alone more enjoyable. For example, consider the situation of a woman who had spent her life raising five children. Her household had been filled with noise and activity. When her children grew up and left home, she found the house too quiet. She spent time with friends but felt lonely when she was home alone. Then she remembered that when she was a child, she had enjoyed cutting up scraps of fabric and sewing them into doll clothes and doll blankets, and she decided to take a course in quilting. She has now completed quilts for all of her grown children and is working on quilts for her grandchildren. She spends every free moment working on her quilts and enjoys her time alone. Furthermore, she has kept in close touch with several people she met in the quilting class and now considers them good friends.

Bob's story provides another good example of the power of looking back at one's childhood for clues on how to spend time alone enjoyably. Bob is in his mid-thirties and recently divorced. He misses his two young children who are with him only part of the time. When he is alone he feels very lonely. He remembered that when he was a boy he had been an avid hiker and fisherman, and had enjoyed woodworking class in school. So he decided to spend some time each week hiking and fishing. Then he purchased some woodworking tools and began building a set of bookshelves. He now finds time alone very rewarding and looks forward to it.

What are some activities that you enjoyed by yourself at other times in your life, even when you were a child?

_____

_____

When could you try doing some of these activities to see if you still enjoy them, and to see if you want to continue doing them to make your time alone more enjoyable? Check those activities that you find you still enjoy and plan to continue doing.

_____

_____

_____

Is there some other new activity you could try that might help you fill the empty spaces in your life? Following are suggestions of some activities people enjoy doing alone. Many of them are inexpensive and some are free. Circle those activities you want to try.

woodworking • needlecraft such as knitting, crocheting, or cross-stitch • photography • art work such as sculpting, painting, pottery, ceramics, etc. • outdoor activities such as bird-watching, hiking, fishing, sports, gardening, etc. • reading fiction, comics, mystery novels, spiritual writings, etc. (Use your public library.) • playing a musical instrument, taking music lessons, building musical instruments, listening to music, singing in choral groups, etc. • dancing—this can be as simple as dancing alone in your living space or you could take lessons and develop some dancing skills • writing—in a journal, poetry, fiction, nonfiction, plays, etc. • fixing or restoring cars or other vehicles • learning something new such as a foreign language, becoming a ham radio operator, or using the Internet • reinforcing skills you already have such as calligraphy, writing poetry, or wood carving • getting "in shape," doing stretching exercises, aerobics, lifting weights, etc. • doing chores you have been putting off such as cleaning a closet or painting the woodwork—something that would give you a sense of accomplishment when it is done

List other activities that you might enjoy doing when you are alone.

_____

_____

You may be like many people who plan to begin integrating a new activity into their lives and never do it. Making advance preparations and plans may help get you started. Use the following checklist and refer to it frequently.

Activity _____

When I plan to try it _____

What I need to do to prepare to try this activity _____

_____

I will make these preparations (when) _____

_____

Activity _____

When I plan to try it _____

What I need to do to prepare to try this activity _____

_____

I will make these preparations (when) _____

_____

Have the equipment and materials you need for these activities readily available so you can use them quickly whenever you want to. One woman in the Loneliness Study says she has a special place set aside in her home for her meditation practice and writing that includes a desk, chair, table, tape player, writing implements, and pillows. Then when she has time alone, she goes to that place and chooses what she will do to occupy herself. You could set up a similar place and keep your things in a basket, box, or drawer, whatever best fits your specific situation.

Making Changes

To learn how to enjoy time spent alone you need to do some planning and take some action. One woman in the Loneliness Study said that she used to "dread" time alone. Whenever she knew her partner was going to be away for several days and she would have to spend the evenings by herself, she felt more and more anxious. Finally, she decided to change her way of thinking about her time alone. She wanted to look forward to this time—and to plan for it. The next time her partner was going to be away for three nights she planned ahead. She decided to spend one night listening to some old jazz records she hadn't heard since she was a teenager. Another night she cooked herself a gourmet meal, and the third night she worked on an art project that she had set aside long ago. Now, she looks at the time she spends alone as her own special time to enhance her life.

In order to enjoy spending time alone, you may need to do the following:

1. Make a list of things you could do during your time alone that would keep you from feeling lonely. You could copy this list and post it on your refrigerator for quick reference at unexpected times alone.

Things I could do when I am alone:

_____

_____

2. Anticipate time alone and plan for it. The following exercises will help you think about planning ahead for time alone.

If you were told that you had to spend the next three days alone in your home because you had an infectious illness that didn't make you very sick, but meant that you couldn't go out, what could you do to avoid feeling lonely?

_____

_____

_____

If, because of transportation problems, you had to spend every evening at home by yourself for two weeks, what could you do during that time to avoid feelings of loneliness?

_____

_____

_____

If you were going to be bedridden for three weeks and would be alone from nine in the morning until five in the evening, what could you do during that time?

_____

_____

_____

3. Change your attitude about spending time alone. Check any of the following negative statements that describe how you feel about spending time alone.

_____ I hate time alone.

_____ Whenever I am alone, I feel very lonely.

_____ Time alone seems to "drag by."

_____ Time alone seems like a waste of time.

List any other negative statements you commonly say to yourself when you are anticipating spending time alone.

_____

_____

To change your attitude about spending time alone, replace the negative thoughts with positive ones every time it comes up. Examples of positive statements are as follows:

Negative Thought	**Positive Statement**
I hate time alone.	I love time alone.
Whenever I am alone, I feel very lonely.	Whenever I am alone, I enjoy myself.
Time alone seems to "drag by."	Time alone goes very quickly.
Time alone seems like a waste of time.	Time alone is good time.

Now, develop positive statements to counteract the negative statements you wrote above.

Negative Thought	**Positive Statement**
_____	_____
_____	_____
_____	_____

4. Addressing your fears.

   Imagine a worst-case scenario. For instance, you are in a cafe sipping tea and reading the newspaper. A man comes up to you and says, "You are alone. That must mean that nobody likes you."

   What could you say in response? You could say:
   "I chose to come here by myself because I wanted to be alone." Or
   "I enjoy being alone."

   Now write some other ways you could respond or things you could say.

   _____

   _____

   _____

   Describe another worst-case scenario related to being alone.

   _____

   _____

   How could you deal with it so it wouldn't be "all that bad"?

   _____

   _____

Additional Activities

Some other activities you could do to increase your enjoyment of time spent alone include the following:

1. Try several of the solitary activities described in this chapter. Do any that you enjoy two more times. Note how you feel when you are doing these enjoyable activities. If you continue to enjoy them, make a commitment to keep doing them on a regular basis.

2. Spend five to ten minutes each day sitting alone and being with yourself. Afterwards write what you thought about during those times and describe how it felt.

3. Make a list of the things you enjoy about being alone like the one that follows:

    I enjoy being alone because I can:
    > do whatever I want to do
    > explore my personal issues
    > play my music as loud as I want

4. Set aside time every week to do something special by yourself, something you don't usually do alone—go to a movie or a concert, go for a walk, have a drink at a cafe, go to a community event, etc. Write about how it felt after you do this.

CHAPTER 5

The Self-Esteem/Loneliness Connection

I always feel so badly about myself. I never thought that anyone would want to be my friend.

—Twenty-nine-year-old man

You may be wondering why there is a chapter on self-esteem in a book on loneliness. The reason is that the loneliness Study showed that two factors are key to significantly reducing or relieving loneliness. They are (1) feeling good about yourself, that is, having high self-esteem and (2) being able to enjoy time alone (discussed in chapter 4).

Low Self-Esteem and Loneliness

From time to time most people feel badly about themselves, that is, they occasionally experience feelings of low self-esteem. This is "normal." However, if you feel badly about yourself most of the time, it may be interfering with your ability to make and keep friends. When you don't feel good about yourself, you usually feel that others won't like you. These feelings keep you from reaching out. In fact, some researchers have found that when you feel better about yourself, you feel less lonely and have more positive relationships with others.

David Burns, in his book *Intimate Connections* (1985, pp. 25–26) says that

> If being alone does not cause loneliness, and if having someone to love is not the cure, then what is the difference between people who feel lonely and people who don't? The crucial difference is self-esteem. . . . Finding someone to love is not the solution to loneliness. The solution is learning to love yourself.

Later in this book he also says,

At the very moment you begin to feel good about yourself, you will start to project positive feelings to other people. They will suddenly sense the love and positivity within you, and they'll be attracted to you. (p. 47)

If your self-esteem is low, improving it will help you to relieve your loneliness. In addition you will see positive change in all the other areas of your life.

Self-Esteem Building Exercises

The following exercises and activities are designed to help you improve your self-esteem. Repeat those that you find most helpful from time to time. Working on improving your self-esteem is a lifelong process. The more you do this kind of work, the better your life will be.

Cost-Benefit Analysis

In this exercise you will look at what it costs you and think about how it benefits you to feel badly about yourself. Then you will look at what it would cost you and how it would benefit you to feel good about yourself.

Write a paragraph that describes your negative feelings about yourself. It can be as long or as short as you want it to be. Use additional paper if necessary.

_____

_____

_____

_____

Reread the paragraph you just wrote.

Ask yourself this question: "How does it benefit me to think about myself this way?" Then write your answer in the space provided below.

_____

_____

_____

_____

Now, ask yourself, "What does it cost me to think about myself this way?" Then write your answer below.

_____

_____

_____

_____

Now ask yourself, "How would it benefit me if I did not think these negative thoughts about myself?"

_____

_____

_____

_____

Ask yourself, "What does it cost me to avoid thinking negative thoughts about myself?"

_____

_____

_____

_____

Review your responses to the last two questions. What have your learned from your answers?

_____

_____

_____

_____

If you learned from this exercise that it will benefit you to think positive thoughts about yourself without costing you anything, cross out the paragraph of negative thoughts to signify that you are going to think about yourself positively from now on.

Self-Esteem Building Exercise

This exercise will help you to discover and reinforce your positive attributes. To do this exercise you will need a piece of paper that is not in this book. Any kind of paper will do. However, if you have a piece of stationery you really like or a sheet of colored writing paper in a color that makes you feel good, that will be even better.

Set a timer for ten minutes or note the time on your watch. Write your name across the top of the paper. Then write everything positive and good you can think of about yourself. Include special attributes, talents, and achievements. You can use single words or sentences, whichever you prefer. You can write the same things over and over if you want to emphasize them. Don't worry about spelling or grammar. Your ideas don't have to be organized. Write down whatever comes to mind. You are the only one who will see this paper. Avoid making any negative statements or using any negative words—only positive attributes qualify for this exercise.

When the ten minutes are up, read what you have written to yourself. You may feel sad when you read it over because it is a new, different, and positive way of thinking about yourself—a way that contradicts some of the negative thoughts you may have had about yourself. Read what you wrote several times. Put it in a convenient place—your pocket, purse, wallet, or the table beside your bed. Read it over to yourself several times a day to keep reminding yourself of how great you are!

Invalidating the Source

When learning to feel better about yourself, it helps to identify the person or people who gave you erroneous messages about yourself, and then to make an accurate assessment of their qualifications for determining how you should feel about yourself.

Who gave you erroneous messages about yourself? Was it relatives—parents, siblings, grandparents, uncles, aunts, or cousins? Were there family friends or neighbors who caused you to feel badly about yourself? Did your schoolmates or your young friends have a negative effect on your self-esteem? Were there people who worked with children, such as teachers, clergy, or activity group leaders who are partially responsible for your feelings of low self-esteem? Perhaps you can think of other people like employers or media role models who may have influenced how you feel about yourself?

Write the name of the person who you think may have damaged your self-esteem and beside it write one or several reasons why that person was *not* qualified to determine how you should feel about yourself. For example, what you write might look something like this:

Name	Reasons Why That Person Is Not Qualified to Judge You
My fourth-grade teacher	She acted like she didn't like kids, she was nasty to everyone in the class.
A high school classmate	She was too young to be able to judge me. She was not nice to lots of nice kids.

Name	Reasons Why That Person Is Not Qualified to Judge You
_____	_____
_____	_____
_____	_____

Based on these assessments, you probably don't want these people deciding how you should feel about yourself. However, it is often very difficult to "let go" of the effect these people have had on your thoughts. The following exercise may help you to diminish or get rid of their influence entirely.

Write the names of all of these people on a sheet of paper. Then choose to do one of the following actions:

- Cut the paper into tiny pieces and throw it away.

- Tear up the paper into very small pieces and throw it away.

- Color all over the paper with a thick black magic marker and throw it away.

You may want to choose a special place to get rid of the paper, such as tossing it in with the garbage, or depositing it in a dumpster or an incinerator. Turn this exercise into a "letting go" ceremony. Many people feel much freer when they complete this exercise. They say it feels as if they have "gotten rid" of the person or people who made them feel bad about themselves—and along with that go the bad feelings about themselves.

Sometimes, you may feel as if you have gotten rid of these people, but then you may notice yourself thinking about them again or about the demeaning things they said to you or did to you. That would be a good time to repeat this exercise.

Changing Negative Thoughts About Yourself to Positive Ones

In this next exercise you will make a list of negative thoughts you have about yourself, and develop positive responses to these negative thoughts. With practice and persistence, you will find that you will think positive thoughts about yourself more and more often.

Begin by listing negative thoughts you have about yourself. You may find this to be very easy for you. Most people do. In the space next to the negative thought, write a positive response that contradicts the negative thought about yourself. The following guidelines will help you in developing these positive statements.

- Avoid using negative terms such as *bad, blame, shame, guilty*.

- Use only positive words such as *friendly, warm, compassionate, responsible*, or *competent*.

- Substitute *it would be nice if* for *should*.

- Use *I, me*, or *your own name* in the positive response.

Examples:

Negative Thoughts	**Positive Response**
I am not a likable person.	I am a likable person.
I never say the right thing.	I often say the right thing.
No one likes me.	Many people like me.

_____

_____

_____

To change the negative thoughts you have about yourself into positive ones takes time and persistence. If you use the following techniques consistently for four to six weeks, you will notice that you don't think these negative thoughts about yourself as much. If they recur at some other time, you can repeat these activities. Don't give up. You deserve to think good thoughts about yourself.

1. Write your positive responses on a piece of paper. Keep them in your pocket or some other convenient place. Read them over and over when you first awaken in the morning. Read them again before you go to bed at night. Read them over and over when you have nothing else to do—such as waiting for the bus, waiting for an appointment, or while riding your exercise bicycle. Read them or say them aloud to yourself or to someone else any time you get a chance. Writing them out one or several times whenever you get a chance also helps. Write them on a sheet of paper, tape it to your bathroom mirror and reread them every time you look in the mirror. You may think of other ways to reinforce these positive responses.

2. Every time you catch yourself thinking the negative thought about yourself, replace it with the positive response.

Make Self-Affirming Lists

Make a list of your five greatest achievements and reread the list often. Here are some examples of self-affirming statements: "I have held my job for four years." "I completed twelfth grade." "I won an essay contest in high school." You can make this list longer—by listing ten, even a hundred or more achievements—by writing it on another sheet of paper.

1. _____

2. _____

3. _____

4. _____

5. _____

Make a list of five ways you can "treat" yourself that don't include food and that don't cost anything, and give yourself one or several of these treats every day. For example, you could take a walk in woods, window shop, watch children playing on a playground, gaze at a baby's face or a beautiful flower, or chat with a friend. As in the previous list, you can make this list as long as you want to by using another sheet of paper.

1. _____
2. _____
3. _____
4. _____
5. _____

Laughing makes you feel good about yourself. Make a list of five things that make you laugh, and do something that makes you laugh at least once every day.

1. _____
2. _____
3. _____
4. _____
5. _____

Take Good Care of Yourself

Low self-esteem may make you feel as if you needn't bother taking good care of yourself. However, if you work at taking good care of yourself, you will find that you will begin to feel better about yourself and that it will be easier for you to make satisfying connections with others.

Here are some ideas of things you can do to take better care of yourself. You may be doing some of them now. There may be others that you need to work on. As you work on improving your self-esteem, you will find that you will continue to learn new and better ways to take care of yourself. As you incorporate these changes into your life, your self-esteem will continue to improve.

Diet

A daily diet is usually considered to be healthy when it consists of: five or six servings of vegetables and fruit; six servings of whole grain foods like bread, pasta, cereal, and rice; and two servings of protein-containing foods like beef, chicken, fish, cheese, cottage cheese, tofu, or yogurt.

Eating healthy food is a gift you can give to yourself. However, you may feel that healthy food is too expensive—that inexpensive "junk" food fills you up more. If this is an issue for you, try to look at this in a different way. A lot of the calories in "junk" food are empty calories. They give you very few of the nutrients you need to feel well. If you take the money you use to buy things like chips, soft drinks, candy, and other sweets and use it instead for healthy foods like fresh fruit, vegetables, cereals, breads, cheese, and yogurt, you will find that you are not spending any more money and that you are feeling much better. Since these fresh foods spoil more quickly than packaged snacks, buy only as much as you can eat before your next shopping trip.

Exercise

Moving your body helps you to feel better and improves your self-esteem. Arrange a time every day or as often as possible when you can get some exercise, preferably outdoors. There are many different things you could do. Taking a walk is the most common. You could run, ride a bicycle, play a sport, climb up and down stairs several times, put on a tape or play the radio and dance to the music—anything that feels good to you. If you have a health problem that may restrict your ability to exercise, check with your doctor before beginning an exercise program or changing your exercise habits.

Do Things You Enjoy

When thinking about taking good care of yourself, include doing things you enjoy. Numerous studies have pointed to the importance of these affirming activities in helping people to feel well and in raising self-esteem. Using a separate sheet of paper, make a list of things you really like to do. Add new things to this list as you think of them. You may want to make a copy of this list to post on your refrigerator door to help remind you of the things you enjoy doing.

Health Care

Obtain good health care for yourself. Perhaps it is a long time since you have had a physical examination, or you may have a chronic or acute health problem that needs attention. You deserve good health care. If you have a good health insurance plan, this won't be a problem. If you don't, or your access to health care is limited, see what services are available in your community that are free or have sliding scale fees that you could afford. Call your local hospital to check on available options. Although it may be difficult for you to access good health care, it is worth making the effort and getting what you need and deserve for yourself.

If you have low self-esteem, you may neglect personal hygiene tasks that would make you feel better about yourself—things like taking a regular shower or bath, washing and styling your hair, trimming your nails, brushing and flossing your teeth, changing your clothes or even getting dressed (you may feel so badly about yourself some days that you never get out of your nightclothes). Also, other people tend to "shy away" from people who are not clean and neatly groomed.

Spend plenty of time with people who treat you well. Avoid people who treat you badly.

Additional Activities to Help Raise Your Self-Esteem

The following activities will also help you to raise your self-esteem.

1. Develop a scrapbook that celebrates you and the wonderful person you are. Include pictures of yourself at different ages, writings you enjoy, mementos of

things you have done and places you have been, cards you have received, etc. Or set up a place in your home that celebrates "you." It could be on a bureau, shelf, or table. Decorate the space with objects that remind you of the special person you are. If you don't have a private space that you can leave set up, put the objects in a special bag, box, or your purse and set them up in the space whenever you do this work. Take them out and look at them whenever you need to bolster your self-esteem.

2. Make an appreciation paper. At the top of a sheet of paper write "Things I Like About _____ [Your Name]." Have friends, acquaintances, and family members write an appreciative statement about you on it. When you read it, don't deny it and don't argue with what has been written—just accept it! Read this paper over and over. Keep it in a place where you will see it often.

3. Do a mutual complimenting exercise with a friend. Get together with someone you like and trust for ten minutes. Set a timer for five minutes or note the time on a watch or clock. One of you begins by complimenting the other person—saying everything positive about the other person that she can think of—for the first five minutes. Then the other person repeats the exercise for the next five minutes. Notice how you feel about yourself before and after this exercise. Repeat it often.

4. Get a good book on self-esteem, read it, and do the suggested activities. See the Resources list in appendix C for suggestions.

5. Make it a point to treat yourself well every day. Before you go to bed each night, write about how you treated yourself well during the day.

Another important aspect of relieving loneliness and developing strong connections with others is the ability to communicate well. In chapter 6, "Building Effective Communication Skills," you will learn how to communicate in ways that enhance rather than break down connection with others.

CHAPTER 6

Building Effective Communication Skills

When I was a kid, I spent most of my time on the streets. We never thought about how we talked to each other. We just yelled at each other. Now I am realizing how important it is to think about how I express myself. I can turn people away, or draw them in by the way I talk to them.

—Forty-five-year-old single woman

Communication Styles That Inhibit Relationships

As a child you may have learned to avoid communicating with others as a way to protect yourself or to make yourself feel comfortable. Or you may have learned negative or indirect ways of communicating. You may find that you have a hard time sharing information about yourself with others, talking about your observations, thoughts, and feelings, and letting others know what you want and need. Lack of communication skills or poor communication skills can cause or worsen loneliness. However, positive changes can take place very quickly when you learn ways of communicating that make it easy for others to understand what you are saying, and when you listen closely to what others say to you. In this chapter you will focus on communication styles that interfere with building good relationships with others, learn about developing positive communication skills that will enhance your connection with others, and explore good listening skills.

Do you think that poor communication skills are an issue for you? If so, describe your communication problems in the space provided.

_____

_____

_____

Before you go on to read about effective ways of communicating, it is important to explore some communication styles that, when used, may increase feelings of loneliness. Some of these may be ways you use to communicate. Others may be ways that some people communicate with you. These styles often separate people from each other and increase feelings of loneliness. They include sarcasm, "dragging up the past," hurtful labels, negative comparisons, threats, and judgmental "you" messages.

If you discover you use some of these communication styles, you can work to change them. It's hard work. You have to be very careful of what you are saying for some length of time. After a while, you will notice that you are not using this style any longer. You will have broken this habit and you may notice that your relationships with others feel better to you.

If others use these communication styles with you, you may decide to ask them to change the way they communicate with you. If they make the change, you will probably feel closer or more connected to them. If they don't, you can decide not to spend time with them or to limit the amount of time you spend with them.

Sarcasm

Sarcastic communications are cutting or bitter comments that make the other person feel bad.

Example: Yeah, you'll do a great job. You always were a big talker!

Write an example of a sarcastic statement below.

_____

_____

Do others often make sarcastic comments to you that make you feel badly? If so, who are they? Write their names below.

_____

_____

When they do this, do you want to be with them?

How do you feel when they make sarcastic comments to you? Now, write how these comments make you feel:

_____

_____

How do you think they would respond if you said something like, "I feel _____
_____ when you make sarcastic comments directed at me. It would be more
pleasant for me if you would not do that."

Or you could restate exactly what they said to you, and suggest another way they
might say it in a more supportive way. Now, write your suggestion below.

_____

_____

Are you going to try this the next time someone makes a sarcastic comment
directed at you?

Do you often make sarcastic comments to others? If so, how do you think it makes
the other person feel? Describe how you think it makes them feel.

_____

Do you want to stop making sarcastic comments toward others? If so, when are
you going to start working on it?

_____

Dragging Up the Past

Dragging up the past means reminding the other person of things they have done
in the past that have not worked out well or that they may feel badly about, rather than
addressing what is happening right now.

Example: I remember the time when you burned the dinner seven nights in a row.
Write an example of dragging up the past:

_____

Do others often remind you of things you have done in the past that have not
worked out well or that you feel badly about? If so, who are they?

_____

When they do this, do you want to be with them?
How do you feel when they do this to you?

_____

How do you think they would respond if you said something like, "I feel _____
_____ when you remind me of things I have done in the past that have not
worked out well or that I feel badly about." Or restate exactly what they said to you and
say, "It would be more pleasant for me if you would not do that."

Are you going to try this the next time someone does this to you?

Do you often do this to others? If so, how do you think it makes the other person
feel?

Do you want to stop doing this to others? If so, when are you going to start working on it?

Hurtful Labels

Using hurtful labels means using words such as *stupid*, *lazy*, *good-for-nothing*, *brat*, *fool*, or *jerk*, to label someone.

Example: You are nothing but a big, lazy, no-good jerk.

Write examples of hurtful labels:

Do others often use hurtful labels when addressing you? If so, who are they?

When they do this, do you want to be with them?

How do you feel when they do this to you?

How do you think they would respond if you said something like, "I feel _____ _____ when you use hurtful labels when addressing me." Or restate exactly what they said to you and say, "It would be more pleasant for me if you would not do that."

Are you going to try this the next time someone does this to you?

Do you often do this to others? If so, how do you think it makes the other person feel?

Do you want to stop doing this to others? If so, when are you going to start working on it?

Negative Comparisons

Making negative comparisons means comparing a person to another person in a negative way.

Example: If only you were thin and pretty like your sister!

Write an example of a negative comparison:

Do others often compare you in a negative way to others? If so, who are they?

_____

When they do this, do you want to be with them?
How do you feel when they do this to you?

_____

How do you think they would respond if you said something like, "I feel _____
_____ when you compare me negatively to others." Or restate exactly what
they said to you. Then say, "It would be more pleasant for me if you would not do
that."
Are you going to try this the next time someone does this to you?
Do you often do this to others? If so, how do you think it makes the other person
feel?

_____

Do you want to stop doing this to others? If so, when are you going to start working on it?

_____

Threats

Making threats means telling someone you are going to hurt them in some way.
Sometimes people threaten other people as a way of trying to get them to do something
they don't want to do. Sometimes threats can be very violent.
Example: If you tell my wife, I will tell the boss you haven't been doing your
work.
Write an example of a threat:

_____

Do others often threaten you? If so, who are they?

_____

When they do this, do you want to be with them?
How do you feel when they do this to you?

_____

How do you think they would respond if you said something like, "I feel _____
_____ when you threaten me." Or restate exactly what they said to you.
Then say, "It would be more pleasant for me if you would not do that."

Are you going to try this the next time someone does this to you? (In some instances this might be too dangerous. Your best option might be to find a safe way to get away from the other person—and then to avoid that person.)

Do you often do this to others? If so, how do you think it makes the other person feel?

_____

Do you want to stop doing this to others? If so, when are you going to start working on it?

_____

Judgmental "You" Messages

Giving judgmental "you" messages means speaking to the other person in an accusatory way.

Example: You are always behind in your work when the supervisor comes in. You always fool around until it's time for the supervisor to arrive. Then you look busy while she's here.

Write an example of a judgmental "you" message:

_____

Do others often use judgmental "you" messages when addressing you? If so, who are they?

_____

When they do this, do you want to be with them?
How do you feel when they do this to you?

_____

How do you think they would respond if you said something like, "I feel _____
_____ when you speak to me like that." Or restate exactly what they said to you. Then say, "It would be more pleasant for me if you would not do that."
Are you going to try this the next time someone does this to you?

_____

Do you often do this to others? If so, how do you think it makes the other person feel?

_____

Do you want to stop doing this to others? If so, when are you going to start working on it?

_____

Other Negative Communication Styles

Describe any other negative communication styles that others use when talking with you, or that you use, that keep you from feeling closely connected to each other.

_____

_____

If others do this to you, do you want to be with them when they do it? How do you feel when they do this?

_____

How do you think they would respond if you said something like, "I feel _____ _____ when you _____ when addressing me." Or restate exactly what they said to you. Then say, "It would be more pleasant for me if you would not do that."

Are you going to try this the next time someone does this to you?

Do you often do this to others? If so, how do you think it makes the other person feel?

_____

Do you want to stop doing this to others? If so, when are you going to start working on it?

_____

Working successfully on eliminating your own bad communication styles takes time, effort, and persistence. But it is well worth it. It is also worth asking others to talk to you in certain ways if it is safe, and to avoid talking to you in ways that make you feel badly.

As you do the things you do every day, in your family, your work, in the community, and at social gatherings, observe how people are communicating with each other. Look for examples of poor communication styles to remind yourself of the changes you are making in your own style.

Clear Communication

When you communicate clearly with others, you increase the possibility of having a positive interaction. By communicating clearly with people to whom you are already connected in some way, like family members, friends, and coworkers, your relationships will be enhanced. When you communicate clearly with people you have just met or know more casually, you will increase the likelihood that you will want to stay connected to each other in some way, or to build a closer relationship. Even if there is no opportunity for you to be connected in the future, you will both feel better about the interaction.

Clear communication styles can be learned and used consistently by understanding (1) the different kinds of communication, and (2) effective communication guidelines. However, communicating clearly requires understanding and consistent practice.

Kinds of Communication

When you communicate with others, you are sharing observations, thoughts, feelings, and needs or wants.

Observation means telling someone else exactly what you saw, heard, read, or experienced. An observation is often a statement of fact. In clear communication you provide accurate observations to the best of your ability.

Here are some examples of clear observations:

It is a warm sunny day.

I shopped at the supermarket on the way home from work.

I heard that the president is going to introduce a new health care bill.

My blue pants are in the wash.

I read a great review about the new movie at the Alhambra.

When you share observations, you share something exactly the way it is or was.

Write three examples of clear observations:

_____

_____

_____

Thoughts are conclusions you have drawn from things you have observed or experienced. They may include value judgments, wishes, and desires.

Here are some examples of thoughts:

I hope it doesn't rain tomorrow.

It's a hard life.

I would have less pain if I did my stretching exercises more often.

I like John because he has a great sense of humor.

Write three examples of thoughts:

_____

_____

_____

Feelings are expressions of emotions. They can be very difficult to share. Other people may not want to hear them. They may act bored or upset when you share your feelings, or they may just hear what they want to hear and ignore the rest. You can decide which feelings you want to share with others and which you do not wish to share. When you share feelings with others, it helps them to understand you, and it may help them to better meet your needs. Share feelings that have to do with the information you are trying to communicate.

Here are some examples of feelings concerning a particular stated fact:

I feel really sad about the loss of my friend.

I get really upset when you are late.

I miss my husband when he is away on business.

I am afraid of thunderstorms.

I am scared when I am alone.

Write three examples of feelings:

_____

_____

_____

Needs. Communicating what you need lets others know what is important to you. This may be very hard for you to do. Many people have a hard time asking for what they need. Often they feel it is bad to ask for anything. It's important to understand that it is often a very good idea to ask for the things you need. When you need something, make straightforward requests. Say exactly what you need. Sometimes, because of habits you may have developed in the past, you may not ask directly for what you need—and then you feel badly when you don't get it. For example, Theresa needed her son to take her to the doctor because she would not be able to drive herself home after the surgical procedure. John needed a ride to school because he missed the bus. Susan needed some good food because her blood sugar was low.

Here are some further examples of needs:

I need to have testing to check my medication level.

I need a warm place to sleep on this frigid night.

I need to eat enough food every day to maintain my blood sugar levels.

I need to get eight hours of sleep every night.

I need locks on the doors so I can feel safe.

Write three examples of needs:

_____

_____

_____

Wants. Sometimes you just want something. It may be something small or frivolous, like a hot dog or a bracelet. Or it might be something big like a new living space or more free time. These "wants" are not necessities.

You don't need them, you just want them. Many people are confused about the difference between needs and wants. You may feel you have no right to wants that are not also needs. Nevertheless, you are entitled to wanting things that will make your life more fun, or easier, or more interesting.

Here are some examples of wants:

I want a warm sweater.

I want someone to walk with me.

I want a new journal for my writing.

I want to have time to draw.

Write three examples of wants:

_____

_____

_____

Clear Communication Guidelines

The following guidelines will help you to communicate more clearly with others. Read them over several times. Then keep them in mind as you communicate with others.

1. Give whole messages that include all the important pieces of information. Don't leave important information out. Avoid sharing so much information about minute details that the other person becomes bored.

2. Use "I" statements like "I feel angry," "I am upset," and "I like being with you," when talking about yourself and your experience.

   Write three "I" statements:

   _____

   _____

   _____

3. Ask yourself the following questions about the communication:

What am I observing, thinking, or wanting in this communication?

What is the purpose of this communication?

Is the stated purpose the same as my real purpose?

What am I afraid of saying?

What do I need to communicate?

Think of a communication you recently had with another person. Describe it:

_____

_____

What were you observing, thinking, or wanting in this communication?

_____

_____

What was the purpose of this communication?

_____

_____

Was the stated purpose the same as your real purpose? If not, why didn't you share your real purpose? What were you afraid of saying?

_____

_____

What did you need to communicate?

_____

_____

4. Watch the response you get from the person or people you are talking to. Check their body language so you can know if this is the right time to be sharing this, or the right subject for this person. You may need to change what you say and when you say it according to the response you observe. Think of a time recently when you were communicating with another person. What kind of response did you get to what you said? What kind of body language did you observe?

_____

_____

Do you think this was the right time to be sharing this with the other person? Do you think you should have changed what you were saying or stopped the communication according to the response you observed? If so, how could you have done that, or how could you do that another time?

_____

_____

5. Depending on the communication, you may want to talk to this person or these people in a private place where you won't be interrupted, a place that is congenial, physically comfortable, and quiet, with few distractions.

The following examples will help you understand the difference between clear and unclear communications:

Unclear Communication	**Clear Communication**
Why won't you hurry up?	I wish you would come right now.
I'm sick of everyone.	I plan to spend a half hour alone in my room now.
You never tell me the truth.	I don't believe you when you tell me things like that.
You are just a jerk.	When you said I wasn't trying hard, it made me feel upset.
You don't know how to dress.	I don't like the color of your dress.
I'm really pissed off.	When you tell me I am not doing my job, I feel angry.

Write some examples of unclear communication and clear communication.

Unclear Communication	**Clear Communication**
_____	_____
_____	_____
_____	_____

Let's take a look at an unclear communication and see how it can be changed so that it is clear, direct, and not likely to arouse confusion or hostility: Jill was working hard by herself on a project that had to be completed to meet a deadline the next day. A coworker came in and asked Jill to help her with another project. Jill responded to the request by snarling, "Why do I have to do everything around here?"

Observation: Jill was working on a difficult project with an immediate deadline when she was asked to help her coworker on another project.

Thought: No one helps me and I can't do another thing.

Feelings: I feel tired, stressed, irritated, and unsupported.

Needs: I need others to understand that I have too much to do right now to help on any other projects.

Wants: I want to be left alone to work on this project so I can complete it in a timely fashion. I want to work on this project until it is completed.

A direct, clear statement to her coworker might be:

"I can't help you with another project right now because I am working on this project and the deadline is tomorrow."

Use the following exercises to analyze several verbal interactions you have had recently. Choose interactions that felt difficult for you. You can make up examples if you can't think of recent interactions. Refer to the example above and to the information in the previous section.

A. Describe an experience you had recently that involved talking to someone about something that was difficult.

_____

_____

What happened or what did you observe?

_____

_____

Describe what you thought and concluded from this interaction.

_____

_____

How did it make you feel?

_____

_____

What were your needs regarding this situation?

_____

_____

Now, write a clear statement you could have used when communicating with that person.

_____

_____

Answer the following questions to check your communication.

1. Have you expressed what you actually know to be fact? ____ y ____ n
   Is it based on what you've observed, read, or heard? ____ y ____ n

2. Have you expressed and clearly labeled your inferences and conclusions?
   ____ y ____ n

3. Have you shared your feelings without blame or judgment?
   ____ y ____ n

4. Have you shared your needs without blame or judgment? ____ y ____ n

5. Have you been able to say what you wanted to say? ____ y ____ n

B. Describe another experience you had recently that involved talking to someone about something that was difficult.

_____

_____

What happened or what did you observe?

_____

_____

Describe what you thought and concluded from this interaction.

_____

_____

How did it make you feel?

_____

_____

What were your needs regarding this situation?

_____

_____

Now, write a clear statement you could have used in communicating with that person.

_____

_____

Answer the following questions to check your communication.

1. Have you expressed what you actually know to be fact? ____ y ____ n
   Is it based on what you've observed, read, or heard? ____ y ____ n

2. Have you expressed and clearly labeled your inferences and conclusions?
   ____ y ____ n

3. Have you shared your feelings without blame or judgment?
   ____ y ____ n

4. Have you shared your needs without blame or judgment? ____ y ____ n

5. Have you been able to say what you want? ____ y ____ n
   Is this way of communicating new to you? ____ y ____ n

_____

Does this way of communicating feel comfortable to you? Why or why not?

_____

_____

What have you learned about communication from this exercise?

_____

_____

Self-Disclosure

Talking about yourself and your experiences to someone who is trustworthy and supportive can help you to build a strong relationship with that person. However, many people are reluctant to share personal details of their lives. You may be afraid that others will not want to hear about your life, don't care enough to listen, or will invalidate or trivialize significant life experiences. You may be afraid that the listener will disapprove of what you are saying or will reject you if he or she knows about your life.

These are valid fears. However, these fears can inhibit your relationships with others. In order to relieve these fear you will have to take some risks to discover who to share with, how much to share, and when to share. The following steps will help assure that your self-disclosure feels good to everyone involved and that it strengthens the bonds that connect you with each other.

1. Consider carefully with whom you will share. Choose someone who likes you, who has expressed an interest in you and your life, and is a good listener.

2. Begin by sharing simple or small things and keeping your sharing brief, increasing the length of time you share and the kind of information you share as you begin to feel comfortable doing so.

3. Let the person know what you want, such as:
   • validation

- whether or not you want feedback and advice
- whether interruptions are okay

4. Make sure the person or people you are sharing with gets equal time to tell you about their lives.

5. Avoid sharing intimate details of your life with someone (a) you have just met or have not known very long, (b) who is likely to share the information with others, or (c) who has treated you badly in the past.

6. If you have something troubling or traumatic to share with another person, be sure it is all right with the other person before you proceed. If it seems to be upsetting to that person, you may want to stop or change the subject. The sharing of troubling or traumatic events is often best saved for your closest friends or a counselor.

The benefits of sharing information about yourself with others include:

1. **Increased understanding of yourself**: Often our thoughts, feelings, and needs are confused until we put them into words. In order for someone else to understand what you are saying, you have to organize your thoughts in ways that also will help you to better understand yourself.

2. **Closer relationships**: Relationships deepen when you share intimate details of your life with someone you care about who also cares about you.

3. **Improved communication**: As you share more openly with others, you will notice that they share more openly with you.

4. **More energy**: Keeping important information about yourself and your life hidden inside you uses up energy. As you share with others, you will notice feelings of relief and higher energy levels.

Describe other benefits of sharing information about yourself.

_____

_____

You might begin the process of sharing the details of your life with a counselor or one or more close friends. You might join a support group where you can share with others who have had similar life experiences. You will find instructions for Peer counseling in appendix B. Peer counseling is a structured way that many people are using to share information about themselves in a safe and supportive manner. Read the instructions and decide if this is something you might want to try.

You may find it helpful to write in your journal about how important people in your life have communicated with you, and how that has affected your feelings about them and/or your relationship with them.

You can learn more about good communications in the book *Messages: The Communication Skills Book* (McKay, Davis, and Fanning 1995). See the Reference section at the back of this book.

Listening to Others

Listening is an essential part of communicating with others. Connections with others need to go both ways. Each person must get a chance to talk and a chance to listen. If one person talks all the time and the other person gets little chance to share, the connection will not be strong. In fact, in the Loneliness Survey many people noted that they tend to avoid people who do all the talking and don't listen well. Do you think you talk too much and don't give others equal time to share?

If you feel this is a problem for you, try to concentrate on being a good listener and giving others equal time to share. You could practice this by being aware of how much time you have to spend with your friend. If it is an hour, make sure each of you get about half an hour to share and half an hour to listen. You could begin the conversation by asking the other person what is going on in his or her life. As they talk, you can ask questions that will encourage them to talk more. Then, when they have talked for about half the time, you will feel more comfortable sharing what you want to talk about. You may want to tell your friend that you know you have a problem with talking more than your share of the time and that you are working to overcome this problem.

Perhaps you feel that you are the kind of person who is very quiet and does most of the listening. If you feel this is a problem for you, tell your friend or supporter that it is hard for you to share with others. Ask them to help you with this problem by encouraging you to talk and asking you questions about the matters you discuss.

Good Listening Guidelines

1. Listen closely to what the other person is saying. Let the other person know you are paying close attention through eye contact, body language, and occasional brief comments like, "I knew you could do it," "That sounds like fun," or "I bet you wish it had happened some other way."

2. Avoid thinking about what your response is going to be while the person is talking.

3. If a person is sharing something intense and personal, don't do something else at the same time that would be distracting, such as clearing the table or washing the dishes.

4. Don't interrupt others when they are speaking.

5. Sometimes it is important to be realistic about how much time you can spend listening and to tell the other person how much time you have. For instance, if a friend wants to get together and talk to you about a problem at work, tell her you have only half an hour, and then you have to do something else. This gives the person advance notice about your time limits and keeps you from having to listen longer than you can. This way you can give your friend more focused attention than if you are wondering when she is going to stop talking so you can get dinner ready.

6. When someone is sharing something intense and personal, avoid adding an "I can top that story" such as "Oh that's nothing compared to the trip I

went on." Respond with comments like, "I'm sorry you have been having such a hard time," "Is there anything I can do to help?", "That must have been really hard," "It sounds like you did a great job," and "I hope it keeps working out well for you."

7. Avoid giving others advice unless they ask for it—just listen.

8. Remember that what people are saying may be important to them even if it doesn't seem important to you.

9. People often need to share the details of hard times or difficult experiences over and over again until they have "gotten it out of their system." You can be a really good friend by listening to the same story again and again. You can reassure them by telling them it is okay to do this.

10. Avoid listening to the following:

   - Accounts of events that upset you. For instance, if someone is describing the details of a horrific motor vehicle accident, it may cause you to become very upset. In that kind of situation, it is okay to ask the other person to change the subject.

   - Comments that make you feel badly about yourself. You can ask to change the subject or leave. If someone tells you how you should change, or is rude to you, no explanation of why you are leaving is necessary. It is up to you whether or not to tell the person why you are leaving.

   - You can choose not to listen to gossip, malicious, or prejudicial talk.

Like many others, you may not always make good use of your listening abilities. You may want to practice listening closely by doing the following activities:

1. Sit quietly and focus on listening to everything you hear—birds singing, the wind, rain on the window, traffic sounds, etc.

2. Focus on listening to all the words of songs you listen to on records or the radio.

CHAPTER 7

Feeling Good About Being with Another Person

I feel good about being with another person when I feel worthwhile, that someone really cares, and that someone is there to talk to when I need to talk.

—Twenty-seven-year-old woman

What does it mean to feel really "with" another person or with other people? What is that like? Many people report that they have never had that experience. Being with another person—both of you being there for each other in a way that feels equal to both of you is often called "mutuality."

Being in a mutual relationship does not mean being in a romantic relationship, though mutuality in a romantic relationship is very positive and necessary. Mutuality describes friendship, the state of actively caring about someone who cares about you in return. There are other kinds of relationships that are not mutual, such as parenting, caretaking (or being caretaken), or volunteering, in which the giving and receiving are necessarily unbalanced, and these too are rewarding when we choose them consciously. But we also need at least some mutual relationships. If you find that you are lacking these in your life, addressing this issue may be an important step in relieving your loneliness. Mutuality is worth striving for. When you are in a mutual relationship with another person (or other people), you feel really good about yourself and the other people you are with; life feels basically okay even though you might be having a very hard time.

Positive Interactions

How do people describe their positive interactions with others? One person in the Loneliness Study said that when she feels good about being with another person she feels *whole*. It is as if a piece of herself that was missing has been found. Others said they felt good about being with another person when they felt they had the unconditional love and support of that person—not *needing* to be together but *wanting* to be together. Words used to describe what such interactions feel like included *comfortable, relaxed, connected, joyful, positive, upbeat, trusting, respectful, spontaneous*, and *honest*. In such interactions affection is expressed but boundaries are also respected.

Mutual, positive relationships include a good mix of speaking and listening where each person communicates fully and is understood. Disagreements are easily and amicably resolved, and both people feel safe to "open up." Each person values the other and respects his/her ideas and beliefs even if they didn't agree. Each person enhances the other. Good laughs together are a great bonus.

Now, describe what a positive interaction with another person means to you:

List the times in your life when you felt well supported, including who was supporting you, and the details of those times. If it would be helpful to you, write on another piece of paper and tuck it into the workbook, or write in your journal.

Time when you felt well supported:

Who was supporting you (one or more people):

Describe the details of that time:

Time when you felt well supported:

Who was supporting you (one or more people):

Describe the details of those times:

Review the information that you wrote about the times when you felt well supported. Were there any specific people who were there more than once? If so, who were they?

_____

_____

Were there any people who were alike in some ways—such as people from your church, people you "hang out" with, coworkers, friends, or family members?

Who   **Attributes**

_____   _____

_____   _____

_____   _____

Are you still connected to these people? If so, do you want to spend more time with them to relieve your loneliness?

_____

If you are not still connected with them, would you like to reconnect with them? If so, when and how could you do it?

_____

_____

Feeling Connected

Many people, from time to time, feel separate and apart from the nice people around them, in spite of their desire to feel close. They often find it difficult to feel connected and close to those with whom they spend time together or with those who share their lives. For instance, a man in the Loneliness Study said, "My family and a few very close friends had gathered to celebrate a birthday. Everyone was having a good time (or so it seemed to me), talking together, laughing, and joking. I was very quiet. No one seemed to notice. I felt left out. I felt like everyone there was more popular and better than I was."

If you have this sense of being unconnected and distant from others all of the time, or even most of the time, you probably feel that you are missing out on an important part of life. You probably want to do something to change this situation so you will feel lonely less often when you are spending time with others.

When you are with others and still feel lonely, many different feelings arise. Noticing and naming these feelings can help you to understand what is really going on during these times. People in the Study noticed the following feelings and thoughts when they felt lonely in a group. Which ones do you relate to? Check off those that apply to your situation.

_____ low self-esteem

_____ lack of self-worth

_____ sadness

_____ separateness

_____ my social skills are poor

_____ no one wants to hear what I have to say

_____ no one really likes me

_____ I don't belong

_____ overwhelmed

_____ I don't have anything in common with these people

_____ no one is noticing me

_____ everyone here is better than I am

List other thoughts and feelings you have had when you were lonely in a group.

_____

_____

Here are two examples of situations where someone felt lonely while with others.

Example 1

Situation	**Wedding Reception for My Niece**
What were you doing?	Visiting with family members and friends I had not seen in a long time.
What were your feelings?	I felt overwhelmed, out of place.
Why do you think that was so?	There were too many people in too small a space.
What did you do about your feelings of loneliness?	I left.
What you could do about it another time?	(1) I could choose to attend smaller or more intimate gatherings; (2) I could take a friend or two along to have someone to talk to; (3) I could look for someone I know and start a conversation with that person; (4) I could offer to help serve refreshments as a way of making a connection with others and to feel a part of things.

Example 2

Situation	**A Party with Fifteen People to Celebrate My Son's Graduation**
What were you doing?	I was serving food, and trying to talk to people.
What were your feelings?	I'm not really part of this group. It doesn't really matter whether I am here. People would have a good time whether I was here or not. Sadness, low self-esteem.
Why do you think that was so?	(1) I think I was starting to get depressed. (2) Everyone was feeling really happy and I wasn't.
What did you do about your feelings of loneliness?	I didn't talk to anyone very much and kept myself busy in the kitchen and serving food.
What could you do about it another time?	(1) Watch for and address early warning signs of depression. (2) Start a conversation with someone who doesn't seem too involved.

In the following exercise, you will look closely at two times when you were with people and felt lonely, including the feelings associated with that time and the possible reasons you felt that way. Then you will devise some alternate ways you might deal with similar circumstances so you will feel less lonely.

Your Situation (1): _____

What were you doing? _____

What were you feeling? _____

_____

Why did you feel that way? _____

_____

What did you do about your feelings of loneliness? _____

_____

What could you do about those feelings another time? _____

_____

Your Situation (2): _____

What were you doing? _____

What were you feeling? _____

_____

Why did you feel that way? _____

_____

What did you do about your feelings of loneliness? _____

_____

What could you do about those feelings another time? _____

_____

Using your personal resources and creativity, you can find ways to increase your feelings of connection when you are with others. When you were doing this exercise, did you notice any patterns in your behavior that might have contributed to your loneliness? Once we notice our patterns, we can choose not to do them. If you noticed any patterns, describe them in the space below.

_____

_____

Barriers to Feeling Well Supported

From time to time you may do things that can keep you from feeling well supported, that is, you may be putting up "roadblocks" or barriers. Everyone does this from time to time. You may know why you do it or you may not. Once you become aware of these barriers, you can choose to raise them less often or not at all, thus enhancing the quality of your interactions with others and increasing the likelihood that you will feel well supported in return.

People often steer clear of someone who has a habit that turns them away or that they find offensive. If people avoid you, you may not even know why they do it. And, if you don't know why people are avoiding you, you can't do anything about it. Of course, people could be avoiding you for reasons that are outside of your control, but if you feel that people turn away from you more often than you would like, it might be important to examine some of your habits. Conversely, if you find yourself feeling uncomfortable with someone in your life, think about what it is about that person that puts you off.

One of the most common barriers to feeling well supported is being in the company of someone who talks incessantly and doesn't give others a chance to converse too. They try to share every detail of what they have experienced or what they are thinking, while their "listeners" become totally bored, even sleepy. If you know someone like this, you probably have observed that you try to avoid this person. Or you may realize that talking continually is a habit of yours. If this is so, and you want to relieve your loneliness, you will want to try to make sure others have as much time to speak as you do. Practice creating some silences in your conversations so that the other person can bring up something on his or her mind. You will also want to learn how to convey the major points of what you are trying to say without sharing all of the details. People in the Loneliness Study described some of the barriers or habits that they felt kept them from feeling connected to or well supported by others. Check off any that you think might be habits you have that act as such barriers. At the end of this section, there are some ideas for taking action so these habits will stop interfering with your connection to others.

Review this list. This may be difficult for you. It's hard to admit that you may have been behaving in ways that turn others away from you. However, if you don't realize that this is a problem and you keep doing things that turn others off, you will never solve your loneliness problem. (Give yourself a special treat when you finish this hard work to remind yourself of what a good person you are.)

If you haven't gotten any ideas about things you do that might be causing people to avoid you, ask someone you trust (e.g., a friend, family member, or counselor) to tell you anything they have noticed that you do that might make people avoid you. Promise that you will simply listen and will not become angry with them or yourself. Then, add any of their observations to your list.

If you still have not gotten any ideas for yourself from this exercise, and if you feel confident that you already have good social skills, you can skip doing the following exercises and move on to chapter 8.

____ being verbally abusive or offensive

____ complaining constantly

____ being self-centered

____ being fearful of rejection

____ having low self-esteem

____ being excessively angry

____ being self-destructive

____ creating crises

____ choosing to isolate

____ worrying and fretting needlessly

____ failing to keep in touch with others

____ heading off rejection by rejecting first

____ being judgmental

____ focusing on the negative

____ violating others' boundaries

____ sharing personal information inappropriately

____ being closed-minded

____ using foul language

____ telling "dirty" racist or ethnic jokes

____ being too loud

____ practicing poor hygiene

____ talking incessantly

____ giving others no chance to talk

____ paying no attention when others are talking

____ giving too much advice

____ interrupting

____ nagging

____ being overly critical

____ teasing

____ having to be right all the time

____ being "bossy"

____ being unsupportive

____ behaving in a clingy manner

____ being disrespectful

____ being dishonest

____ being unreliable

____ being irresponsible

____ betraying confidences

____ flirting with others' partners

____ being argumentative

____ being bad tempered

____ calling other people names

List any other things you do that you think might turn others off:

_____

_____

_____

Breaking Down the Barriers to Feeling Well Supported

If you have identified some behaviors that might be contributing to your loneliness, you will want to change the way you do things and/or stop doing certain things. At first, you may want to work on only one or two of these, and go back to the others at a later date. Here are some ideas that may prove helpful to you. Which of these will you follow?

Tell a close and trusted friend or counselor about the behavior you are trying to change and what you plan to do about it. Ask that person to support you in creating this change by asking you every once in a while how you are doing and praising you for doing well.

Becoming aware of what you are doing that turns others off is often enough to keep you from doing it in the future. Fill in the following commitment statements with descriptions of the behaviors that you want to change and think you can change simply by deciding to stay conscious of the need to do so. Read Exercise 2, Cost/Benefit Analysis, to learn how to do a cost/benefit analysis for changing these behaviors.

Exercise 1: Commitment Statements

I (offending behavior) _____ ,
which makes others want to avoid me. Therefore I am going to stop doing it.

I (offending behavior) _____ ,
which makes others want to avoid me. Therefore I am going to stop doing it.

I (offending behavior) _____ ,
which makes others want to avoid me. Therefore I am going to stop doing it.

Cost/benefit analysis _____

Exercise 2: Cost/Benefit Analysis

Perhaps in order for you to change your behavior, you need to study it closely. This exercise will help you do that. Here is an example followed by space to do a cost/benefit analysis of one of your behaviors.

Example

First, describe the behavior you want to change:

I want to stop lying.

Ask yourself the question: "How does it benefit me to do this?"

It makes me feel better about myself for a little while.

Now ask yourself, "What does it cost me to do this?

Other people don't trust me and they don't want me to be with me.

Now ask yourself, "How would it benefit me if I did not do this?"

If I didn't lie, people would trust me and want to spend time with me.

Ask yourself, "What would it cost me if I did not do this?

Nothing. Or perhaps some minimal short-term embarrassment, which would be tiny compared to the benefit of long-term trust.

Now, review your responses to the last two questions. What do you conclude from your cost/benefit analysis?

More people might want to spend time with me if I didn't lie. I would probably have more friends and I wouldn't be as lonely as I am now. In any case, I know that good long-term relationships aren't possible if I continue to lie, and I think I can handle the temporary embarrassment of stopping lying.

Use the following form to do a cost/benefit analysis of one of your behaviors. The behavior I want to change is

_____

How would this behavior benefit me?

_____

What does this behavior cost me?

_____

How would it benefit me if I did not do this?

_____

What would it cost me if I did not do this?

_____

_____

Review your responses to the last two questions. What do you conclude from your cost/benefit analysis?

_____

_____

Repeat this exercise for other behaviors you want to change.

Doing the Opposite

When you are tempted to do something that you know turns others off, turn it around and do the opposite. For example,

- If you feel like saying something critical to another person, compliment him or her instead.
- If you feel like flirting with your sister's husband, spend some time talking with your sister instead.
- If you feel like blowing smoke when you are talking to someone, put your cigarettes away.
- If you feel like skipping your shower even though you really need it, take your shower.
- If you feel like clinging to someone, do something you enjoy doing by yourself.

To practice this technique, write an opposite behavior for each of the behaviors listed below:

- If you feel like whining, you could _____
- If you notice you are talking incessantly, you could _____
- If you are quiet and never share anything, you could _____
- If you don't listen to others, you could _____
- If you feel like nagging someone, you could _____
- If you feel like using foul language, you could _____
- If you feel like telling a "dirty" joke, you could _____
- If you feel like being very loud, you could _____
- If you feel like complaining, you could _____
- If you feel like sharing something someone told you in confidence, you could

  _____

- If you feel like being critical, you could _____

Goals and Rewards

Set a goal for yourself and reward yourself when you have met it. For instance, you may want to stop being critical of others. You could put a dollar (or a quarter) in a jar for every day that you manage to go for the whole day without criticizing anyone. When you have put a dollar (or any amount you feel comfortable with) in a jar every day for two weeks (or whatever time you want to set as your goal—it could be shorter or longer depending on how long you think it will take you to break the habit and what you want for your reward), use the money to buy yourself something you have really wanted—like a new blouse, an audio or videotape, a poster, a plant, dinner at a special restaurant, and so forth.

- You could put a sticker or star on a calendar for each day you avoid using foul language.

- You could treat yourself to a movie after avoiding particular behavior, such as not having a temper tantrum, for a week.

- You could ask someone to do a chore for you, such as cooking dinner, after you have avoided nagging for a week.

What is your goal (related to changing behaviors that turn others off)?

_____

How are you going to reward yourself when you meet this goal?

_____

What is your goal (related to changing behaviors that turn others off)?

_____

How are you going to reward yourself when you meet this goal?

_____

Finding Support

Your problem may be so difficult to deal with that you want to enlist the aid of a supportive counselor. Many insurance programs will cover all or some of the costs of this counseling. If you think you need this kind of counseling, and it is not available to you through your insurance program, or the cost is prohibitive, call your local mental health agency to see if they have any free or low-cost services to offer. Also see the list of self-help books in appendix C, "Resources," at the back of this book.

Watch Other People for Clues

Practice watching other people's body language to help you learn how to recognize what another person may be trying to tell you by the way he or she acts. Do this by watching people interacting with each other. Note to yourself those times when you think these interactions are positive and you think that the people you are watching feel mutually supported. Also pay attention to those times when barriers keep people from being close to each other. If you want to, you could write about these interactions and describe what you learn from them.

Maintain Contact

Relationships need attention to flourish. If people don't stay in close touch, often the relationship will wither and die. Make it a point to stay in regular contact with people you care about—those with whom you want to have an ongoing relationship and who help to relieve your loneliness. Call, write, or email them often. Arrange regular times to get together. For instance, you could both agree that you will get together one afternoon a week to go for a walk or that you will call each other every Friday morning. My elderly father stays in close touch with his sister by calling her every Monday morning. Even though they are don't live close enough to see each other, this contact keeps their relationship strong and supportive. They both look forward to this time together. Sticking to a regular time can be very enriching to a relationship, even if it is occasionally difficult to do.

Peer Counseling

Peer counseling is a structured form of mutual support that will provide you with partners and structured times to practice changing the habits that may be sabotaging your connections with others. In peer counseling, two people get together regularly for a specified amount of time. The time is divided in half with each person having equal time to share and to listen to the other person. Complete instructions for peer counseling are included in appendix B.

Be Realistic

Be realistic about your expectations. Behaviors that you have had all your life are often very difficult to change. Don't expect change to be accomplished overnight. As you work on creating this change, write in a journal to remind yourself of your progress. It's hard work, but it offers great rewards.

Appreciating Change

As you begin to make changes in the way you interact with people, you will begin to notice that you feel less and less lonely. In addition, you may notice other positive changes in your exchanges with others and in the way you feel about yourself. For instance, one woman in the Loneliness Study said that as she began making changes in the way she interacted with others she began to feel more self-confident. Another said, "The feeling is the indicator—you feel good." Other responses addressed feelings of security, comfort, ease, acceptance, understanding, and validation.

A woman in the Study spoke of the new sense of mutuality in a significant relationship. She said, "When I have a good talk with my friend, she can talk about her good and bad and sad stuff. I can listen and cry or laugh with her. Then we turn it around and I can share my stuff with her. I feel supported when I feel I have something to give the other person too." This view was supported by a woman who said, "There's give and take in my connections with others. We smile and laugh together. We advise and help each other. We respect and love each other. There is honesty and trust in our relationship."

Write a statement that expresses how you feel or hope to feel when you begin to create a greater connection to others.

Now we'll do a brief exercise to help you absorb the meaning of the statement that you just wrote. Sit in a comfortable position. Take a few deep breaths. Then focus all of your attention on the statement you wrote above for five minutes. Ponder its meaning. Write how you feel after you do this.

_____

_____

_____

CHAPTER 8

Reaching Out

I have been getting out to groups and various activities. I meet people I am interested in getting to know better all the time, but I just don't know how to take the relationship to that next step—where we become friends.

—Thirty-seven-year-old single man

If you believe that your loneliness is primarily or partly caused by the lack of close friendships in your life, then you will almost certainly need to start reaching out to make connections. Connecting with new and/or old friends can be exciting or intimidating, depending on your personality and your circumstances. But certainly it will be ultimately rewarding.

The first step in reaching out is meeting people who might become friends. As you get to know them, you will find that some are more interesting to you than others, that you share some common experiences, or that you enjoy sharing news and gossip with each other. These are the people who gradually become your friends and supporters. Where do you connect with these people? How do you proceed when the connection is made?

Meeting new people who might become your friends doesn't usually "just happen." It takes action. People don't often come to your home searching you out. You have to go where they are. If getting out to meet others is difficult for you because of a special life circumstance such as a disability, refer to chapter 15, "The Challenges of Loneliness."

If you can get out easily and you live in an area where there are lots of activities, you can look for ideas in local newspapers or other publications, make some choices, and take some actions.

The woman in the following story is an excellent model for "getting out there." Gretchen was seventy-eight-years old when she moved from her condominium in a friendly town in Vermont where she had lived for ten years to a residential area in a big city. She has moved several times in her life, and each time she has worked hard at making connections.

I've made several moves to new towns. And in the past I always looked for a tennis club first thing. Not for social reasons or to avoid loneliness. But, as it turned out, my favorite sport served as a perfect "entry" into a new social setting. I met compatible people and made lasting friendships. Alas, I can no longer play tennis! So I had to find another group to join. This wonderful city has so much to offer and the newspaper is full of suggestions. I've checked out whatever seemed interesting and suitable. Among other things I've joined a great church, registered for art classes and lectures at the art museum, subscribed to a concert series, joined walking and cruising tours to learn about the history and culture of the city—filling my days with enrichment and enjoyment. So I live alone which has good features and bad. And I am not young which is too bad (!) and also I have vision problems and some hearing loss. But one can still make things work by following up leads and talking to people about what they like. And most importantly, it feels good to get out and enjoy the world.

Looking Back

You may have enjoyed going to a place in the past—a place where you connected with people and made friends. But you stopped going for some reason and never started up again. For instance, a few years ago I would spend every Friday evening at a folk dance. I did that for several years. I felt welcome there, enjoyed the dancing, and made many new friends. I had to stop going because I had surgery. After I had recovered I often thought about going back, but I never got around to it.

Are there some places you have enjoyed going in the past but no longer go—places you could go again? If so, list them here:

_____

_____

_____

Searching for Ideas

Where can you get ideas on places to go and meet people? People in the Loneliness Study listed the following ideas. You may be able to think of some others.

1. Ask friends, family members, acquaintances, coworkers, and health care professionals for ideas.

2. Refer to listings in regional and local newspapers.

3. Radio stations often feature listings of community events (call them to find out what time these listings are aired).

4. Local or public access television stations may show listings of community events.

5. Various agencies in your community may be able to give you referrals, such as the local senior center, a volunteer coordinating agency, the chamber of commerce, health care agencies, universities, colleges, community colleges, and adult education programs.

6. Read signs posted in store windows, grocery stores, laundromats, restaurants, health care agencies, health food stores, on phone poles, and kiosks.

If you have any other ideas on how to meet new people list them below:

_____

_____

What Are Your Options?

Many communities offer a broad range of activities, special interest, and action groups. These may be open to the public or accessible by becoming a member. Like others, you might look through the newspaper and say to yourself, "That would be a fun and/or interesting thing to do. . . ," and then you don't follow through. You don't go to the event. The hardest thing about going out and doing *anything* in the community is going the first time. Don't think you are alone. It's hard for everybody. Push through those hard feelings and go. Most of the time you will be glad you did.

Most communities offer a wide variety of interesting and entertaining events and activities where you can go and meet others. Following is a list of ideas. After you have read them, write down any events or activities that you would like to attend, adding any others that you can think of. Don't limit yourself to one idea or strategy. The broader your effort, the greater your likelihood of success. For instance, one person in the Study said that all his friends had been connected to him through his workplace. When he retired he felt very alone. While continuing to keep in touch with some of his colleagues from work, he found he had to work at rebuilding a new network of friends and supporters.

Sporting events (spectator or participant)	Attend or participate in a play
Attend or participate in a concert	Art galleries, shows, and museums
Poetry readings, book signings	Special interest groups
Civic groups	Activist groups working on specific issues
Political party meetings	Church
Gym	Walking tours

Now list the community activities and events that are of interest to you:

_____

_____

_____

Some possibilities deserve special attention because so many people said these had "worked for them"—that they had found friends and supporters in these places and situations. These possibilities are discussed below.

Classes

Isn't there something you'd like to learn? Take a class. Study a foreign language, computer science, bird-watching, knitting, wood carving, literature, pottery, whatever interests you. Many classes are inexpensive or free. Inquire whether scholarship aid is available. The classroom situation and shared interests make a class an excellent place to meet new people.

Classes I might enjoy: _____

_____

Volunteering

There are many agencies that could use your help. Inquire at churches, schools, hospitals, youth agencies, soup kitchens, the Red Cross, etc. Many communities have agencies that organize volunteers and would be a good resource if you are looking for the right place to volunteer. Some newspapers also run listings of volunteer opportunities.

When you are volunteering, you have an opportunity to meet others with common interests while doing something useful that you enjoy doing. Regular contact and working together encourages the development of supportive relationships. Working for the benefit of others also tends to take your mind off your own problems and loneliness. Remember, the more you learn to give, the greater your capacity for receiving becomes. Read through the following list of volunteer options. Make a list of those that appeal to you and add any others you can think of.

hospitals • public service agencies • nonprofit organizations • libraries • schools • community programs • Big Brother or Big Sister programs • hospice programs • youth programs

Volunteer options I could explore:_____

_____

Support Groups

Joining a support group is a great way to connect with others who have interests and issues similar to yours—people who might become friends. Many years ago I did a study to find out how people who experience distressing symptoms, such as depression or anxiety, deal with these symptoms and get on with their lives. One of the questions I asked in that study was, "How have you built a support system for yourself?" An overwhelming number of people said they did this through regular attendance at a support group. Support groups often counter the social isolation that causes people to feel lonely.

Many of the people in the Loneliness Study liked support groups because in such groups they are treated as "equals." There is mutual sharing and understanding. Group members validate each other's experiences. Often there is a level of trust found in these groups, established by the group, that does not exist in other situations, making it safer to be vulnerable and reach out. It's great way to connect and share with others who have similar experiences. One woman said, "The group increases my understanding of and empathy for others, which makes me a better friend."

The following story illustrates how a support group can meet very special needs—needs that sometimes had not even been articulated. One woman said:

> *I belonged to a women's group for a couple of years. On many occasions we would express our appreciation of one another. One time we were writing our appreciations on index cards. Several people mentioned how they appreciated my patience and calmness. However, although I know I appear to be calm and self-controlled, I experience restlessness and anxiety going on quietly pretty often. Because I was trying to be open with these women, and because they only saw one layer deep, I was pricked with feelings of isolation, loneliness, and "invisibleness." But then, one of my better friends in the group gave me her card which had deeper insights, and said more things. One thing she mentioned was my "precision." No one had ever said this to me, but I related to it immediately—it's what I strive for when I want the details to be right. I keep her index card within reach on a shelf near my bed. I can talk with this friend about pretty much anything and everything.*

Another example of the effectiveness of support groups was shared by a woman in college. She went to her support group at college after a very difficult weekend with her family. She said:

> *When I returned to school after the wedding, I was confused and in a weird funk . . . feeling about as much a misfit in my family as I ever had, and my attitude was showing all over. At that night's session, I was asked to explain my feelings so that the group could talk about it. That night turned into one of the most emotionally intense bonding sessions for a group of people that I have ever been a part of. We collectively cried, expressed outrage at society's view of minorities, hugged each other, and talked about our collective sense of detachment from other people because we were "different." The following week was a time of belonging for all of us. No one wanted to see it end. It gave me a glimpse of what it could feel like to belong to something and have friends who understood me in a deeper way, the way that I truly craved to be understood.*

Almost every one has a hard time going to a support group for the first time. Sometimes it is difficult to force yourself to go even if you enjoy the group and have been attending for some time. Excuses like the following keep people from attending:

I'm too tired when I get home in the evening. • I'm fearful of meeting new people. • I'm afraid I won't be liked. • I'm afraid I won't be welcomed. • It feels very risky. • Transportation is difficult. • It's hard to get a ride. • I can't find a group that seems to fit me. • I don't like to tell others what's going on with me.

You may need to address your issues. Think them through and do a cost/benefit analysis (see chapter 7). Or maybe you can "just do it." But however you get past that first hurdle, you are likely to find attending a support group richly rewarding. Different kinds of support groups include the following:

women or men • people of certain ages, such as a group for women in menopause or men who are retiring • special needs or conditions, such as caregivers, cancer patients, diabetes patients, weight loss dieters, people with addictions, or those dealing with bereavement • special circumstances such as having a parent with Alzheimer's, being recently divorced, or being a crime victim • people with common interests such as books, bridge, hiking, and bird-watching

List the kinds of groups you think you would be interested in:

_____

_____

_____

It is wise to attend a support group several times before making a decision about whether it is the right one for you. Every group can have an off night where things just don't "gel." You will know whether this is not the right group for you if, after a few meetings, you still feel like an outsider. Don't give up! Search out another group.

If you can't find a support group that you meets your needs, you may want to start one of your own. It's not a difficult thing to do. Setting it up with another person makes the process easier and more fun. There are many options for groups and there is no one "right way" for a group to be. There is specific information about starting a support group in appendix A.

If you are going to attend a support group and connect with the other people in the group, you must feel safe there. Many groups address this need by having a set of guidelines or rules for the group—sometimes called a safety contract. Group members first discuss what they need in order to feel safe in the group and then someone writes up a list of what has been agreed upon. The list can be posted somewhere in the meeting place, passed out to new members, or read aloud to the group before each meeting. Although this list varies from group to group depending on the purpose and focus of the group, the following list details some of the most common needs:

- **Confidentiality**. (1) There must be a clear understanding that personal information shared in the group will not be shared with anyone outside of the group. (2) Group members will not tell people outside of the group who attends the group.

- **Sharing**. (1) There will be no interrupting when someone is speaking or sharing. (2) Everyone gets a chance to share but you don't have to share if you don't feel like it.

- **Criticizing**. Judging, criticizing, teasing, or "put-downs" are not allowed.

- **Giving Feedback**. Group members give other group members feedback only when it is requested.

- **Comfort Level**. Group members may leave the group whenever they want or need to take care of personal needs, to be comfortable, or to attend to other responsibilities.

- **Attendance**. Attendance is optional.

You may want to keep this kind of commonsense safety contract in mind in other realms of your life, too. There are certain courtesies and implicit contracts in friendships, and we are less likely to violate them if we are conscious of them.

Workplaces. It is common for people to develop close connections and friendships in their workplaces. You may find people at work who share your interests and experiences. In addition, you are together much of the time. It's convenient. You might get together before or after work, eat lunch together, and check in with each other throughout the workday.

Places to avoid. There may be some places you want to avoid when you are looking for new people to become part of your life. If you have gone to some of these places in the past, you may be tempted to go back and try again. If you are tempted, be sure you review the reasons why you started avoiding these places before making a final decision. Some reasons for avoiding certain places might include these:

- You have had bad experiences there before, e.g., people don't welcome new arrivals.

- They support addictive behaviors, e.g., you are a recovering alcoholic and people drink there.

- It is not safe, e.g., there have been several muggings in the area.

- People of questionable intent and character hang out there.

- You have disturbing memories of experiences at that place.

List those places you want to avoid when you are looking for potential friends.

Beginning Steps

Reaching out to people who seem interesting to you and who seem like potential friends is hard work. Building your self-esteem will ease this process. One fifty-five-year-old woman in the Loneliness Study put it this way:

At one time I made a list of potential friends and acquaintances and called each person. I made small-talk conversation and then in a straightforward manner told the person I would like to renew our friendship and invited them for lunch. This continued for over a year and was a fun experience. I had grown apart from these individuals, and renewal of our mutual affections was a usual result.

How are you going to know that another person might be interested in being your friend? Assessing this question carefully will help you make the most effective efforts. If you are especially sensitive to the discomfort of rejection, even if it is only someone telling you they haven't time to get together with you, it is an especially good idea to think through who is sending you signals that they may be potential friends. Before you "reach out" to a particular person, you may want to consider the following questions:

1. Watch what's happening. When they are with you do they seem friendly? Do they smile a lot? Are they interested in what you are saying? Do they seek you out when you are in a group? What does their body language tell you?

2. Is it reasonable to expect that this person would want to become friendlier with you? For instance, if you are taking a college course, it might not be reasonable to expect to have a friendship with the instructor or professor. It also might not be reasonable to expect a very busy parent of several small children to have time for another friend.

3. Do you and this person share some interests in common?

4. What is there about this person that makes you want to establish a friendship? Do you have a good reason, like you enjoy being with them and talking to them? Or is it not a good reason, like accruing prestige for yourself or getting a job you have been wanting? Avoid insincere reasons as they are likely to set you up for disappointment.

How Are You Going to Reach Out?

How do you take an acquaintance to the level of a friendship?

One person in the study said: "I met Holly at a meeting of volunteers to plan a local Earth Day celebration. Holly and I volunteered to work together setting up a series of hikes in our community. As we worked together planning the hikes, we realized we had many interests in common. She suggested we begin hiking together on Thursday afternoons and I eagerly agreed. Now, ten years later, we no longer have time for weekly hikes, but we get together regularly over lunch and share what we want to of our lives. We know we are there for each other, even when we aren't together."

Have you ever reached out and successfully established a friendship with an acquaintance? If so, it may help you to recall how you did it by writing about it, so you can do it again.

_____

_____

_____

Reaching out to establish a friendship often happens simply and casually. But if you feel you need to take some action to turn an acquaintance into a friend, you could do any of the following:

• Invite your acquaintance to join you at a cafe for coffee or lunch.

• Ask the person to go for a walk or engage in a sport with you.

- Call your acquaintance on the phone to share a piece of good news you think might interest him or her.

- Invite the person to attend an event with you that is connected to the one where you met or where you have been seeing him or her.

- Talk with your acquaintance about something of mutual interest (you can get ideas on what might be of mutual interest by thinking about where you met, e.g., if you met at a bird-watchers group you could share information on a recent sighting and ask if they had made such a sighting).

- Offer to help the person with something if it is clear your help would be appreciated.

What are some other ideas you have on how you could turn an acquaintance into a friend?

_____

_____

_____

What Turns the Other Person "Off"

I was really enjoying chatting with her at the meetings. Then she started calling me several times a day. She told me all her troubles. I had a hard time getting off of the phone. She found out where I lived and started stopping by. I couldn't get anything done.

—Twenty-four-year-old single woman

People in the Loneliness Study were asked, "What would keep you from wanting to become friends with someone you have met?" The most common reason given was that that person did all the talking and did not listen, or that such a person did not listen long enough or attentively enough. The people in the Study also often mentioned other people constantly interrupting when they were trying to talk about something. One woman in the Study said, "I really do believe that many lonely people are 'unpopular' because they have never learned to listen and to take part in a dialogue. As my daughter says about my friend, 'He says, "Hi, how are you doing," and you have thirty seconds to tell your story. The rest of the time is his.'"

One woman said she had a friend who talked constantly whenever they got together or whenever she called on the phone—and *never* listened. This woman knew everything that was going on in her friend's life, but her friend knew nothing about what was going on with her. Finally, it stopped feeling like a friendship. Then the woman who did all the listening took a risk, interrupted her friend's monologue, and said, "You have been talking now for over half an hour and I haven't had a chance to speak. I know everything about your life and you know nothing about my life." Her friend gasped in amazement. When her friend had recovered from her shock, she thanked this woman for her honesty and said, "Sometimes I notice people's eyes 'glaze over' when I am talking." The two women then made an agreement that, when they get together, each person would have half the time to share—much the same as in peer counseling. Since that time their friendship has flourished.

When you are reaching out to change the nature of a relationship from acquaintance to friendship, the relationship could end abruptly if you:

- Talk too much and don't listen to the other person.

- Keep the discussion focused on yourself and don't pay attention to the other person.

- Try to get too close too fast and expect too much too soon.

- Overwhelm the person with calls, notes, cards, and requests.

- Discuss very personal information too soon.

- Ask for "favors" like baby-sitting or to borrow money before the relationship is well established.

- "Beg" the other person to be your friend because you are so lonely.

Thinking about what others have done that made you afraid of becoming more closely involved with them will help you to remember what you want to avoid doing. List any other behaviors you can think of that turned you off someone.

_____

_____

_____

These are things you need to keep in mind as you reach out. Your outreach will have greater chances of success if you proceed slowly, keeping both your needs and the needs of the other person in mind. If you slip up, forgive yourself and refocus on the feeling of caring.

Fear of Rejection

Thinking about reaching out to explore a friendship with another person—taking that first step—is not easy. It tends to bring up lots of fears, the most common being the fear of rejection. You may be afraid that, if you reach out to the other person, that person might let you know in some way—either subtle or obvious—that he or she is not interested in getting to know you any better.

Have you ever tried to reach out to someone in the past and been rejected? If that ever happened to you, how did it make you feel?

_____

Because being rejected can leave us feeling badly in some way, a common response is to avoid reaching out or to do it with great caution. Although this attitude is common, it is very limiting and can contribute greatly to loneliness. This is a situation where many people "pull themselves up by their bootstraps," assess the situation, and try again. The following exercise might give you an idea of how to proceed.

Exercise: Cost/Benefit Analysis

One way to convince yourself to reach out again is to do a cost/benefit analysis exercise. You may recall you did such an analysis in chapter 7 to help you change some behaviors that may be impeding your search for friendship. In this instance, you can do a cost/benefit analysis to determine whether to reach out to others.

In this cost/benefit analysis, you look closely at (1) the *costs* of reaching out and (2) the *benefits* of reaching out as a way of deciding whether you want to reach out again. Begin by asking yourself, "What does it cost me to reach out to someone?" Your response might be "Nothing," or it might be "Risking being rejected and hurt." What would your answer be?

_____

What is the benefit of reaching out to someone? Your answer could be, "I might have a new friend or I might not have a new friend." What would your answer be?

_____

Your thoughts might be, "If I make a new friend, that would clearly be a benefit. Relieving my loneliness is important to me. If it doesn't work, I won't have lost anything, or maybe I might feel badly about it for a short while." What would your thoughts be?

_____

_____

You may have decided you want to "let go" of or ignore your fear of rejection and reach out to others who seem as if they could become good friends as one way to relieve your loneliness. If you are committed to reaching out to others as a way to ease your loneliness, the next section will help you develop the courage to do that more easily.

Finding the Courage to Reach Out

To reach out to others, you have to know that there are good things about you that would make other people want to be with you. Everyone has positive attributes that make them attractive to other people. However, in order to have others appreciate your positive attributes, you have to know that you have them—and act as if you know you have these special qualities. What is there about you that would make other people want to be your friend? What assets do you have that would make you a good friend? Use the following list for ideas and add any others you can think of, then write down the assets and strengths that you would bring to a friendship in the space provided:

I am a good listener.

I am warm and friendly.

I like being part of a good conversation.

I am supportive of others.

I have a lot of interests I like to share.

I am passionate.

I am entertaining and witty.

I make it a point to affirm and validate the experiences of others.

I accept others as they are. I don't try to change them.

I enjoy sharing fun and interesting activities with others.

I am very compassionate.

I am playful and enjoy humor.

I am generous and kindhearted.

I am interested in a variety of ideas, issues, and activities.

I will go "out on a limb" for others if they need and want me to do that.

Now, list your strengths and assets that make you a good friend.

_____

_____

If you have a hard time remembering your positive attributes, even though these are qualities you know you have, reinforce your belief in them frequently. Then, you can reach out to others with the confidence that comes from feeling good about yourself. You can reinforce these positive aspects of yourself by:

- Reading your own list over and over. You may want to copy it onto a separate sheet of paper that you carry with you or leave it posted in a convenient place. Then read it before you go to bed at night, when you first get up in the morning, and anytime you think of it or have a few extra moments.

- Making copies of your list and hanging them on the mirrors you usually look at. Every time you look in the mirror, read the list. You could also hang a copy of the list on the refrigerator door and read the list every time you open the refrigerator.

- Asking someone you know and like to read you the list several times. You could also read it aloud to that person.

- Asking someone you trust to add any positive attributes they see in you and add them to your list.

The likelihood that you will meet people who might become your friends increases if you have a wide range of interests and if there are many different things you enjoy doing. These interests can enhance your life. You will find ideas on interests you might develop by reviewing chapter 4, "Enjoying Time Alone." What interests do you have that you could develop that might bring you into connection with others?

_____

_____

_____

_____

CHAPTER 9

Boundary Issues

The closer he got, the more uncomfortable I felt. I just wanted him to back up and keep his distance.

—Thirty-two-year-old woman

As you work to relieve your loneliness, boundary issues will become apparent to you. When nurturing relationships, if these issues are not handled with care, your best efforts may be wasted.

What Are Boundary Issues?

You learned about boundaries when you were young. When you were an infant and a young child, you gradually learned to identify those people with whom you felt comfortable, and chose to spend time with them, staying away from those with whom you felt less safe and comfortable. If you found yourself with people who did feel uncomfortable or unsafe, you clearly let others know how you felt by crying loudly until the situation was changed to your satisfaction. You responded with pleasure or laughter to some kinds of touch while vigorously protesting any touch that didn't feel good to you. You learned from your experiences and from observing others whether or not they wanted you to come close to them.

Feelings within yourself (intuitions) let you know who you wanted to be close to and who you wanted to avoid. But, as an adult, it's sometimes hard to know what your feelings are trying to tell you. Therefore, boundaries, limits in relationships, can be a difficult issue. They are often hard to define or describe. For that reason, it's frequently hard to know what your own boundaries are, much less to recognize another person's.

Although it is easy to say that friends need to respect each other's boundaries, this is often easier said than done. You may find yourself asking yourself questions like these: "Have I called too often this week?" "Have I stayed too long or should I leave now?" "Should I offer to help her with the children or would she be uncomfortable with that?" "Is it okay for me to go to tea with his wife or would he be sensitive about that?"

"Should I hug him before I leave?" "Is it okay to pat her on the back when she's done something special?"

One person in the Loneliness Study said, "I love having close friends. But when they try to interfere in my family life, or they want me to spend time with them instead of with my wife or the kids, it's not okay with me." Another said, " I don't want friends dropping by any time. I like my personal space. I want a telephone call first." An older man said he didn't want anyone to feel dependent on him. "I want to know that my friends have other people they can call on when they want companionship or have some need. I don't want to be the only one." A woman said, " I shut down when someone who is supposed to be my friend tells me how I should change. Good friends should accept you the way you are." One young woman said, "I need a good night's sleep, so don't call me after nine P.M."

Boundaries differ from person to person. You may feel comfortable with one person calling you whenever he or she feels like it, and want to put some restrictions on calls from someone else. You may not want to go to certain kinds of activities with some friends and be perfectly happy to go to the same activity with others. For example, you might choose not to attend a ballgame with someone who enjoys shouting at the players during the game—but you might enjoy going to a movie with this person.

One way to keep violations of boundary issues from destroying a relationship is to discuss them. Ask other people what's okay with them. They can ask the same of you. For instance, if you would like to get together every week or so for coffee, check it out with your friend. See how he or she feels about it. If they say every week is too often you will need to work together to come up with times that are acceptable to both of you. Find out if it's okay to call before calling each morning to see how things are going. Ask your friend if she minds whether you ask her husband for advice on a financial matter.

Most people commonly set limits or boundaries around matters like:

the amount of time spent together • where time together is spent • duration and frequency of phone calls • amount of support given • advice • connection with family • amount of physical touch

Can you think of anything else you might need to set boundaries around in a friendship? If so, write it down and remember it.

Reading Body Language

The ways people interact and discover each other's boundaries often depend on their skill at read body language, that is, the way we communicate by means of body movements, posture, and gestures rather than with spoken language. Sometimes body language is very clear, such as a disapproving frown or supportive gesture. At other times it is very subtle and it can be more difficult to interpret, a slight change in posture, a way of walking, a blink of the eye. For example, you may be able to tell simply by looking at the way someone stands or walks that it would be acceptable to ask that person for directions.

You can use body language to tell another person what you do or don't want. Body language can provide clues about another person's intentions and what that person does or doesn't want, things like:

do or don't come any closer to me • do or don't touch me • do or don't talk to me • do or don't disturb me • do or don't share a deeper level of intimacy with me

Sometimes you may not even be able to say what it is about someone's body language that sends you a very clear message. However, it is often unnecessary to put feelings that have been conveyed by body language into words in order to take action. Such actions are based on strong instincts or intuitions that were activated by the other person's body language.

Exercise

Suppose you were sitting on a park bench with another person. Without using words, how could that person let you know that he or she would like to get into a conversation with you?

_____

_____

How could that person let you know that he or she did not want to converse with you?

_____

_____

The person might let you know by smiling or nodding at you, not moving away from you, and perhaps looking in your direction from time to time. If the person had some things on the bench, he or she might clear some space for you to sit down. You might also notice that the person seemed comfortable and relaxed with your presence. If that person did not want to converse with you, your presence would not be acknowledged. You would be ignored. And the person most likely would move away from you and look in any direction that prevented eye contact between the two of you.

Touching

Touching is a boundary that is a very sensitive issue for many people. You have the right to touch others or be touched in ways that feel comfortable and safe to you. You also have the right and responsibility to not touch others or be touched in ways that are uncomfortable or hurtful to you. You have the right to say "no" to any uncomfortable touch.

What kind of touch is usually acceptable to you from a family member?

_____

From a close friend?

_____

From a casual acquaintance?

_____

If you feel that you are unclear about what kinds of touch are okay with you, the following exercise will help you to learn how to identify wanted and unwanted touching. Choose several of the following incidents related to touch or write others you can think of and, in the section on the right-hand side, note how the touch felt to you.

Exercise

How did you feel when:

Incident	How It Felt
A baby caressed your face	_____
Your mother hugged you	_____
A dog or cat rubbed against your legs	_____
You gently rubbed your own face	_____
A friend hugged you	_____
Someone you did not know well hugged you	_____
Your partner kissed you	_____
Someone walking on the street brushed against you	_____
Someone you did not know put his or her hand on your shoulder when you were conversing	_____
A cashier inadvertently touched your hand	_____

What did you learn from this exercise?

_____

_____

_____

Making Personal Choices

Sometimes people in close friendships and relationships have to give up some personal choices and work collaboratively with each other to figure out what they are going to do together, and to make other decisions about their friendship. For instance, you may have to let go of your choice of what you are having for dinner from time to time to accommodate your friend's tastes or you may have to change your plans so that the two of you can spend time together.

A healthy relationship is never controlling. There are some choices you must make for yourself alone, even though others may try to influence or control you. When others try to influence you and make your choices for you, it is important to let them know that these choices are up to you. They may include important lifestyle issues such as these:

whom you live with • whom you are intimate with • whom you marry • whether or not you will have children • who your friends are • where you live • the kind of education, work, or career you pursue • the kind of clothes you wear • how you style your hair • how you spend your time • what you eat • how you care for yourself • what you do with your leisure time • what your hobbies and special interests are

Now, list some other life choices that are up to you to make:

_____

_____

_____

If someone else is making these choices for you—or trying to—you can set boundaries in your relationship and make the necessary changes to take back control of your life. Good relationships, the kinds of relationships that relieve loneliness, are not based on control.

In some cases, you may want to separate yourself permanently from a person who is trying to control you—like an unsupportive spouse whom you no longer love. In other cases, you may reduce the time you spend with controlling people or set clear limits about what is okay and what is not in your time together.

Make no mistake, these are not easy tasks. Freeing yourself from a controlling relationship takes courage and persistence, working on small steps to reach bigger goals. (You may consult with a supportive friend or a counselor as you make these changes, but the final decision should always be up to you.)

In setting personal boundaries and creating such changes, it helps to ensure that your interactions with others are positive. This can be accomplished if you are meticulous about using "I" statements. These are statements that describe how *you* feel—not how the other person feels.

For example, if your partner has been telling you that you cannot change jobs, you can merely say, "I want to change jobs and I am going to change jobs." If your partner wants to engage you in a discussion about why you need to keep this job, you can just return to your "I" statement, saying "I am going to change jobs." You can give some further explanation such as, "This job is too hard on my back," or "The hours are too long," but all you really need to say is "I am going to change jobs."

When you are using "I" statements, it is essential to avoid saying anything negative about the other person such as, "You are being unsupportive," or "You don't understand the situation," as this can make the situation much more difficult. In this instance, it is important to keep your needs uppermost in your mind.

Here are some examples of "I" statements:

- I am ending this relationship.

- I am buying myself a new pair of slacks.

- I want the house to be quiet from 9 A.M. until 7 P.M.

- I will not hug you.

- I will not wash the floor.

- I am taking a course at the community college.

- I am getting safe housing for my family.

- I will take a shower before I go to bed.

- I will talk to my friend on the phone for as long as I want.

Dealing with Boundary Violations

If someone violates or tries to violate your boundaries, making you feel uncomfortable, you can take action to change the situation. Depending on the situation and what you feel comfortable doing, you can do any of the following:

1. Tell that person how you feel, what is okay and what is not okay. For example, you might tell an uncle who is always trying to kiss you that you do not want to be kissed by him or that you do not want him to touch you at all. You can tell an acquaintance that you are uncomfortable being hugged by him or her.

2. Avoid the person (or people) who cause you to feel uncomfortable or unsafe. Stay away from places where they might be. For instance, if you don't like being around people who have been drinking, avoid places where alcohol is served. If a relative mistreated you in the past, avoid attending events where that person might be present. Avoidance is *not* a cop-out! It is a totally acceptable way of protecting your boundaries.

3. If you are inadvertently in contact with someone who makes you feel uneasy or even scared, leave the place as quickly as possible. After such an encounter, you may notice that you feel uneasy and unsettled for some time. If this happens to you, it may help to relieve those feelings by sharing how you felt with a trusted friend or a counselor. If you have no one with whom you feel safe sharing the incident, write about it in your journal.

4. If someone violates your space or hurts you, and does not stop when you tell him or her to stop, do whatever you need to do to get away from that person as quickly as possible while keeping yourself safe. Depending on the seriousness

of the incident, contact your local women's crisis center, law enforcement officials, or mental health agency for support and assistance, and, possibly, to initiate legal action for further protection.

Remember, you have the right to:

- Define your own limits and boundaries.
- Spend your time the way you choose.
- Feel comfortable and safe.
- Ask, expect, and insist that others respect your physical boundaries.
- Protect yourself from unwanted closeness and contact.
- Determine how and by whom you want to be touched.
- Say "no" to anything you don't want to have happen to you or to do, and the right to ask for what you need, want, and deserve for yourself.

Now, write about any relationship boundaries you know you have:

_____

_____

_____

Do they differ from person to person for you? If so, how and why?

_____

_____

Are there boundaries that you need to share with others as your relationship deepens? If so, what are they?

_____

_____

_____

CHAPTER 10

Dealing with Bad Relationships

I can't leave this relationship. If I do I know I will never find another friend.

—Forty-five-year-old woman

People who attend workshops on developing and keeping a strong support system often ask this question: "What can I do about my family member or some other person in my life who is treating me badly?" One answer to that is, "Stay away from those who treat you badly." Some people in the Loneliness Study said that they stayed in relationships or friendships where they were often treated badly because they were afraid they would be lonely if they left the relationship. They were afraid that others would not want to spend time with them and that no one else would ever want to be with them. When they finally left the relationship or limited their contact with the people who were mistreating them, they found that they were happier and that, by taking positive actions on their own behalf, they were able to build new friendships and relationships.

One woman in the Loneliness Study said that she had spent many years in bad relationships, as well as having to deal with family members and people at her workplace who frequently treated her badly. She knew that this was making her unhappy and adversely affecting the quality of her life. Yet it was difficult for her to make the changes that would limit or end her contact with these people.

She believed that she couldn't get along without them, and that she might be even lonelier than she was if she avoided these people. Finally, she made it a high priority to spend time with people who treat her well and make her feel good about herself. Gradually she worked her way out of a long-term relationship and explored other options for friendship. She found a new job where people treat her well and appreciate her work. Joining a women's support group got her involved in a variety of community activities. Now, she spends little time with family members who treat her badly and she has a strong circle of good friends. She has married a man who treats her very well and they have a mutual and supportive relationship.

Of course, there are times when you don't have to leave the relationship or avoid the person who is treating you badly. By working together, it may be possible to resolve the situation. For instance, one woman in the Study was going to leave her husband because he often had rages that frightened and demeaned her. Then, they decided to see a marriage counselor. Working together they have gradually resolved the problem and their marriage is now healthy and strong.

In this chapter you will look at (1) issues that can interfere with intimacy and trust in a relationship, (2) how to resolve problems within relationships, (3) how to deal with abusive relationships, (4) how to recognize danger signs in new relationships, (5) how to say "no," and (6) how to identify some thought patterns that may be keeping you from making positive changes in your life.

What Interferes with Intimacy and Trust?

There are many issues and behaviors that can get in the way of intimacy and closeness, causing at least one and often both of the people in the relationship to treat each other badly. Substance abuse—the misuse of alcohol, "street drugs," or prescription medications —is one of the most common. If someone is abusing substances, he or she is often unreliable and has lost the ability to be intimate. Substance abusers may behave in ways that are hurtful or cause you to feel unsafe.

Some other things that can get in the way of intimacy and trust are as follows:

illness • distance • stress • overwork • fear • financial problems and poverty • differences in values and morals • differences in expectations • differences in interests • lack of mutual commitment to the relationship

Now, list issues and behaviors that you think would make it difficult to remain in intimate connection with another person.

_____

_____

Resolving Problems in Relationships

Because each situation is different, you will have to tap into your resourcefulness along with using good communication skills and other strategies to decide what to do and what action to take each time a difficult situation comes up, or you become aware of a difficulty that is preventing the relationship from being intimate and trusting. Some things you can do include the following:

- Talk to the other person using mostly "I" statements.

- Work with your partner or friend to develop a plan to resolve the situation that will include the steps each of you is going to take and when you are going to take them (check in with each other often about your progress).

- Say "no" when necessary.

- Do a reality check with yourself—ask yourself what it really happening here and decide on solutions that will work for you.

- Be clear about your boundaries.(See chapter 9, "Boundary Issues.")

- Discuss the situation with supporters such as friends and counselors.

- Join Al-anon or some other support group where issues similar to yours are discussed.

If you are in a relationship that is not intimate and trusting, and you wish it were, but you do not feel it is safe talking to the other person about it, you may want to discuss this with a counselor, a person who works at a crisis center, or a close friend, to figure out what to do. You may decide for yourself that you want to limit the amount of time you spend with that person or those people.

If you cannot resolve the situation, you may want to end the relationship. This can be a very difficult thing to do. You may have become financially dependent on each other, share a living space, and even have children together. Take small steps. Reach out to others for assistance and support as you work through this process.

It is important to remember that you deserve to be treated well and that you have a right to an intimate and trusting relationship. Many people in the Loneliness Study said they would prefer to be alone than to be in a relationship that is not intimate and trusting.

Dealing with Abusive and Dangerous Situations

Staying in an abusive relationship is a terrible way to avoid loneliness. You should never allow yourself to be mistreated or abused in any way. You are in a bad or abusive relationship if the other person:

- Is not respectful of you, and does not treat you with dignity and compassion.

- Hurts you emotionally, physically, or sexually. Or if that person forces you to do things against your will or threatens you or others closely connected to you, such as your family members, friends, or your pets.

- Is critical and/or judgmental by teasing, ridiculing, or putting you down, or by invalidating your ideas and dreams.

- Tries to control you by making decisions for you and insisting on being in charge. Or puts you under a lot of pressure to do things her or his way.

- Is very jealousy and possessive. Checks up on you, accusing you of flirting and interrogating you about your casual interactions with others.

- Tries to keep you from your friends, family, and other activities.

- Blames you for his or her own problems or actions.

- Has violent rages or has demonstrated very unpredictable behavior.

To keep yourself and others safe as you try to create some distance from such a person, if necessary, you can get assistance and support from a trusted friend, a counselor, or from your local law enforcement officials. All of this may sound very hard. But it is the best thing to do as soon as you can possibly do it. Remember, your life will get better. You will find new friends and supporters and new ways to ease your loneliness.

Danger Signs in New Relationships

Sometimes there are important reasons to avoid becoming closely involved with some people. For example, you may become acquainted with someone and feel there is the possibility of a closer friendship or even an intimate relationship or partnership. Then, if you begin to feel some discomfort with the relationship, you may decide that you do not want to become further involved with this person or these people. But sometimes it's hard to notice when a friendship or relationship is starting to go badly, especially if you really want the relationship to work.

If you have had few friends in your life, you may be tempted to pursue the relationship in spite of seeing one or several danger signs. However, most people agree it is better not to have a friend than to have a friend who treats you, her- or himself, or others badly. One older woman in the Loneliness Study had been in several relationships with men that she had thought initially were going to be intimate, mutual, and trusting. After she had been with each of these men for a time, they became abusive—threatening her and trying to control her life. She found that she was becoming more and more reluctant to even go out on a date.

She finally decided to create a list of "red flags" for herself—clues that would help her to see that a relationship would not be good *before* she got too involved and before it became difficult or even unsafe to leave. If you have been in unhealthy relationships, you may want to develop such a list for yourself. The following list may help you determine what your own red flags should be. These would be the signs that tell you not to get further involved with a person or group because such a connection would be difficult, troubling, not rewarding, or even abusive. It would not help to relieve loneliness but only add further difficulties to your life. Most people feel that the earlier you notice these danger signs and back away from the relationship, the easier it is for everyone involved.

"Red Flags" for Relationships

rudeness • sharing personal information about others • doing all the talking and not listening to others • violation of your boundaries • "know it all" behavior • putting others down • teasing, ridiculing, taunting; and making threats • "badmouthing" your friends and family • lying or being dishonest • wanting you to be their only friend or wanting you to spend all your time with them • flirting with your partner • controlling behavior—wanting to know where you are, who you are with, and what you are doing • not wanting to be seen with you in public places • clinging or very needy—wanting you to take care of them • talking inappropriate sexual talk • leering • making you feel "creepy" • asking questions that make you feel uncomfortable • abusing substances • engaging in criminal activity • wanting you to take care of him or her

What would you put on your list of red flags that would let you know that you need to back away from a new relationship with a potential partner or friend?

_____

_____

_____

Use this list as a guide when you are considering entering into a new relationship.

Sometimes you can end such a relationship simply by discontinuing contact with the person. If the person is insistent that you stay in close touch, you will need to tell him or her that you do not want to do that. You do not need to explain why. If the person persists in trying to stay in touch, you may need to get help from a counselor in finding the best way to end this connection.

You keep yourself out of bad situations with others by avoiding indiscriminate dating, casual or promiscuous sex, and spending time in bars and other places where people might expect something from you that you don't want to give.

Saying "No"

Many of us say "yes" much more than is in our own best interests. Some people say they have a very hard time saying "no" or refusing a request. In addition, you may have a hard time telling others how you feel and expressing feelings of anger. You may have a hard time feeling that you are disappointing anyone—while at the same time you are really doing a disservice to yourself. However, there are times in your life when you need to say "no," or be firm or insistent about what is and is not all right with you. Not saying "no" when you really want and/or need to say "no" can get in the way of your relationships with others.

For example, Jack asked Molly to watch his dog while he worked one Saturday. Molly doesn't like dogs and she had other plans for that day. But she said "yes" to Jack's request because she doesn't like to say "no." By the time Jack got home, Molly was very irritated with him indeed. It took her several weeks to get over the anger she felt about this. It would have been much better for their relationship if she had said "no" to Jack, and told him that she was uncomfortable with dogs and had other things that she wanted to do during that time.

If you have a hard time saying "no" when you would really like or need to, you may have to get some experience in saying "no." Practice saying "no" over and over again every time you have a chance—in front of the mirror, when you are cleaning your living space, when you are driving, or anytime you have some free time. Say it aloud. If no one is around, you may want to shout it—"No, no, no, no!"

You may want to explain to the other person why you are saying "no." However, if you don't want to, you don't have to. Jut saying "no" should be enough.

Sometimes when you say "no," the other person will try to talk you into whatever it is they want. Don't argue with them or try to convince them that your way is right. If you are clear that the answer must be "no," just keep repeating "no" over and over again. If this is hard for you, it may help you to repeat this affirmation: "No one can talk me into doing things I don't want to do, or that are not okay with me."

Here are some examples of when "no" is the only thing you need to say:

- When you can't do what is being asked of you.
- When you don't want to do what is being asked of you.
- When you are asked to do something that is not safe.
- When you are asked to do something that is not in your best interests.

Now, list some other times when "no" is all you need to say:

_____

_____

_____

List times in the past when you wish you had said "no" or where someone convinced you to change your mind and you wish you hadn't.

_____

_____

_____

As an adult, you may find that you want to say "no," but you are afraid that the results of saying it would be unsafe. You may feel you can't say "no" to things like the following:

uncomfortable or intimate touching • sex • doing favors • lending money • medical procedures • abuse and/or harassment • controlling behaviors by others • spending time with people who treat you badly • alcohol or drugs • going places you don't want to go • doing things you don't want to do

Now list some other things you may have a hard time saying "no" to:

_____

_____

_____

_____

When you first realize that you can say "no," it feels very different and very new. For instance, a young woman who has had a hard time in her life saying "no" recalls an incident that she feels was a milestone in her life. She was at a college fraternity party.

The same man kept asking her to dance over and over. Each time she danced with him, she felt more and more uncomfortable as he made more "suggestive" advances. When he asked her to go to his room, she did something that was unusual for her—she said "no." He called her a tease, but eventually he walked off and asked someone else to dance. She was a bit shaken, but she felt very relieved.

Describe a time that you said "no" that you feel good about:

_____

_____

Describe a situation where you have not done things you have wanted or needed to do for yourself, or have let others push you around because you were afraid of what might happen if you said "no."

_____

_____

What could have happened if you had said "no"?

_____

_____

What would have been better—saying "no," or having the "other thing" happen?

_____

_____

How could you have taken control and said "no" without getting hurt or suffering some other negative consequence?

_____

_____

You may have discovered some ways to avoid the need to say "no" while still getting what you want for yourself. That is, you may have learned how to take some actions to get the results you want without directly telling the other person "no." If so, describe what you do here:

_____

_____

You may want to practice saying "no" to someone you have a hard time saying it to by staring intently at a photo of that person (or a picture you draw of that person) and saying, aloud "no, no, no," over and over again. If possible, ask a friend to stay with you when you do this. It is very empowering. You can repeat this exercise whenever you feel as if you are having a hard time saying "no."

Negative Thought Patterns

You may have some negative thought patterns that keep you connected to people who treat you badly or keep you from addressing difficult issues in your friendships or relationships. By thinking about examples of negative thoughts related to dealing with relationship issues you may learn some new ways of thinking. Furthermore, you may discover some new ways to resolve such problems. Listed below are some fairly common thought patterns and other ways of thinking about them that can help you to change negative thoughts to positive ones.

Thought pattern: *I could never leave him. I would be so lonely.*

Another way of thinking: *If I left him, I could do some good things for myself and meet some new people to relieve my loneliness.*

Thought pattern: *This breakup is so humiliating. How can I face people? How can I tell them what happened? What will I do when they ask me where she is? Suppose I start crying?*

Another way of thinking: *This breakup is the best thing for me. It doesn't matter to me what other people think. And I don't have to tell them what happened or where she is. It's okay to cry if I feel like it.*

Thought pattern: *I could never make it on my own.*

Another way of thinking: *I can make it on my own. Lots of people do.*

Thought pattern: *I can't trust anyone. I should have known better than to get in this relationship.*

Another way of thinking: *While there are some people I can't trust, there are also many people I can trust. Most people make mistakes about relationships from time to time.*

CHAPTER 11

Deepening and Sustaining Friendships

It felt so good being together. Such rich time for both of us.

—A woman in her sixties

If you are fortunate, there are people in your life whom you have known and loved for a long time. You may not see them for months or even years. And yet, when you get together, it feels as if you haven't been separated at all. If you have people like this in your life, these relationships are a great gift. Most of our connections with others need more time and attention to stay strong, rich, and vital, to grow, and to be sources of emotional sustenance for relieving loneliness.

In chapter 8 you looked at the many ways you can meet people who might relieve your loneliness and with whom you might develop long-term friendships. But meeting new people is just the first part of banishing loneliness. Keeping the connections with those you meet strong and healthy is work that continues all through your life. You may consider it the most important work you do. Many people do.

This chapter is devoted to the issues related to *maintaining* your connections with others after you have moved past the point of being mere acquaintances. One person in my study referred to this as "courting a friend, or a dance of action." Deepening connections with others takes a long time. You will want to proceed very slowly. If you make one close friend in the next year, that will be a remarkable accomplishment. Long-term friendship takes commitment, trust, and time out of our busy lives.

Recognizing the Right Person

Hopefully, you have already begun doing the preliminary work to relieve your loneliness and your circle of acquaintances has widened. Not all of these people will become close friends. Some will always be people to whom you just say "Hi" when you meet and perhaps chat with for a few minutes.

So, how are you going to recognize a person with whom you will develop a closer bond? Sometimes the recognition is more closely related to a feeling you have when you are with the person than to any specific attributes he or she might have. For example, a man said to his wife, "I know you and my sister will really 'hit it off.' You have so much in common." Yet the relationship never 'got off the ground'—the man's sister remained cold and aloof in spite of the commonalities the two women shared. In another situation, a very poor woman who had little in common with her wealthy, well-educated neighbor found that, when they began taking walks together, their friendship bond grew strong and deep in ways that neither could have ever anticipated.

Some people think your closest friends should not be people who are very different from you. However, people who seem to be very different from each other often make the best of friends. If you limit yourself only to connections with people who are similar to you, you will miss out on wonderful opportunities for closer friendships. In many cases, differences enhance rather than detract from relationships.

Are you are holding on to any prejudices or erroneous thoughts you might have acquired earlier in life that are preventing a potential friendship from deepening? For example, you might be saying to yourself, "Oh, I wouldn't want to be friends with him or her because of _____ (fill in one of the reasons from the list that follows)."

This list will help you to check yourself for any limits you may be placing on potential friendships that you might like to reconsider.

- **Age**. Someone who is many years older or younger than you are can become a strong and wonderful friend. For instance, a fifty-year-old woman said that one of her deepest connections is with an eighty-year-old woman who supported and inspired her when she remarried, developed a new lifestyle, and learned to play the piano.

- **Gender**. Many women report that their very best friend is a man, and many men report having very close connections with women, with no sexual involvement or expectation in either case. One man in the Loneliness Study said that all of his closest relationships are with women.

- **Sexual preference**. Many heterosexual people report rich connections with people who are homosexual—again with no sexual involvement or expectation. Sexual preference issues do not preclude close connections between people.

- **Ethnic background**. People from a wide variety of ethnic backgrounds have become lifelong supporters for each other.

- **Educational background**. The years of education and number of degrees someone may have are not valid yardsticks to determine whether that person is suitable for close friendship.

- **Experiential background**. Even though your life experiences may differ drastically from another person's, strong connections may develop.

- **Religious beliefs**. Unless you and the other person feel you need to convince each other of the superiority of your respective paths, there is no reason that people of different beliefs can't be great friends. Furthermore, sharing information about your beliefs can make for very good conversation.

Now, write any prejudices or erroneous thoughts you think you may need to let go of in order to allow some of your relationships to deepen.

_____

_____

In matters of friendship, listen to your heart. It is usually the best indicator of how to proceed. Commonality of life circumstances may not be as trustworthy. Using narrower criteria, such as common interests or backgrounds, may blind us to the richness right within our reach.

It is never possible to know with certainty whether to pursue a deeper friendship with someone. Test the waters by proceeding slowly. As you both enjoy each other, the relationship deepens. If you have never had a close friend, you may have a hard time knowing when to take action that will allow your relationship to deepen. Watch for the following feelings that indicate a relationship is becoming closer. You will feel the following, to a much greater degree:

- comfortable

- content

- at ease

- unselfconscious

- good about yourself

- enthusiastic

- accepted

- disappointed when you and the other person can't get together

It's also important to be aware of how the other person feels when he or she is with you. You can find out by watching the other person (noticing body language) and other responses, or by asking them.

Sometimes it is helpful to tell the other person that you are interested in establishing a closer connection or deeper friendship. Other times you may choose not to address the possibility of becoming closer friends and just wait and see what happens.

Taking Risks

Sustaining any friendship takes action. You must do something. Sometimes it's not easy to do something. Shyness about calling someone and asking him or her to share an activity is a common problem. Many people experience this. When it's time to make the call they go through a list of "what ifs," such as, "What if they don't want me to call?" or "I am calling them at a bad time."

Use common sense about when you call someone, but don't get caught in a web of indecision. It's important to realize that most people are just wishing someone would call them. Since it is more likely than not that the other person will be pleased that you called, you are not taking a great risk, but it is, nevertheless, a risk. If the other person seems pleased that you called, great. If he or she does not seem pleased that you called, you may have caught them at a hard time, or they might not be interested in furthering the connection with you. Perhaps you should try another time. Or call someone else. Reassure yourself that there are plenty of other people who will be interested in connecting with you. If your early attempts do not yield success, think through what the problem might be, but don't give up. Remember all the things about yourself that make you a desirable friend.

When forming new friendships, another risk you take is bringing up matters that are personal or sensitive in nature. One person in the Loneliness Study called these "soulful topics." In both of these instances—whether to call in the first place and whether to divulge personal information in the second—you take the risk and then you watch what happens and make further efforts based on what you learn. You will find that you can't talk about some topics with some people. For example, some people don't want to discuss personal topics such as the state of their health unless they know you very well. However, they may be wonderful people to go fishing with. Remember, one person will not be able to meet all of your needs for friendship and companionship.

The Qualities of Good Friends

You need and deserve at least several people in your life with whom you have deep, rich friendships. Participants in the Study used the following phrases to describe good friends. They are people:

> You like, respect, and trust, and who like, respect, and trust you. • You feel good being with. • Who listen to you without sharing personal information about you with others, and to whom you can tell "anything." • Who allow you to talk freely and express your feelings and emotions without judging, criticizing, teasing, or putting you down. • Who give you good advice when you want and ask for it, and who work with you to figure out what to do next in difficult situations. • Who allow you the space to change, grow, make decisions and make mistakes. • Who accept you—both as you are and as you want to be. • Who share fun activities with you. • Who have time for you.

You probably can think of other things you need in your friendships. One person in the Study said, "It's nice to have one or two things to disagree on to keep it interesting." List other things that are important to you in relationships with others:

_____

_____

_____

Now, describe your relationships with people with whom you feel you have deep, rich friendships. These are the people you would call if you broke your leg, or if you needed a meal or companionship, and they would probably reciprocate. If you feel you don't have any deep, rich friendships, write what you would like in a deep, rich friendship or skip this exercise.

Person _____ **Relationship** _____

Why do you feel this is a deep, rich friendship?

_____

_____

Person _____ **Relationship** _____

Why do you feel this is a deep, rich friendship?

_____

_____

Mutuality

Friendship needs to go two ways. In any friendship it is important for each person to be there for the other. Both people in the friendship need time to talk and time to be heard. Friends take turns in suggesting activities. From time to time, each calls the other. For example, if a childless person watches her friend's children occasionally, then the parent needs to returns the favor by doing something special for the childless person.

When one person does all the giving and the other person does all the receiving, their relationship is headed for disaster. The person who is doing all the giving will eventually get tired of the relationship and begin to feel "burned out." And for the person who is always on the receiving end the relationship will lose its richness and appeal.

Of course, there are always times in a friendship where one person has a greater need—for example, if he or she has experienced a profound loss or a serious illness. A close, mutual friendship can get through such difficult times easily. For instance, one person in the Study gets together with a good friend several times each month over lunch. Over time, they informally divided their time in half, always paying attention to each other's needs and concerns. However, when one person was rejected by her partner of many years, at these lunches with her friend, she was freely given much more time to share her feelings than was usual.

Do you feel you have mutuality in your friendships? If so, describe how it works or doesn't work.

_____

_____

_____

What Prevents Relationships from Deepening?

Many people have issues in their lives that make it hard for them to develop close connections with others. Some of these issues are listed here along with suggestions for how to resolve them so they don't keep you from effectively deepening your friendships. If the suggestion doesn't feel right to you, talk to a counselor or a good friend about other possible solutions.

Problem: You have been hurt so much you feel that you can never trust anyone enough to feel close ever again.

Possible solution. Remind yourself that you know the danger signs of a bad relationship and can leave whenever you see these signs. Remember that you have the strength to get through disappointments as you have in the past, and that pursuing this friendship might enrich your life.

Problem: You feel that because you don't like yourself, no one else will.

Possible solution. Try to understand that even though you don't feel good about yourself right now, others still like you. Then work on raising your self-esteem. For ideas on how to raise your self-esteem, see chapter 5, "The Self-Esteem/Loneliness Connection."

Problem: You are oversensitive to any sign of rejection and react to it by giving up on the other person.

Possible solution. Avoid giving up on people until you are absolutely sure they can't be supportive. Talk to the other person about what you are feeling, and encourage him or her to share their feelings. Work together so you can both feel good in the relationship.

Problem: You have not had the opportunity to develop the social skills necessary to make and keep friends and supporters.

Often, poor social skills that might create problems are the same kinds of behaviors you might find offensive in others. These include the following:

being overly dependent or needy • expecting too much • lack of attention to others' needs • blaming and "bad mouthing" others • gossiping and spreading rumors • being negative • chattering constantly • expecting the other person to carry all the conversation • being inattentive when others are talking • invalidating others' feelings • lacking good personal hygiene • using foul language • lying • competing or "one-upping" • ignoring boundaries • refusing to share feelings

What do you do or avoid doing that you feel gets in the way of deepening your friendships?

_____

_____

_____

Possible solution. Just recognizing that you have this problem is taking a giant step in the direction of resolving it. Once you have recognized the problem, you can work on correcting it by avoiding or changing the behavior. You may want to design a reward system for yourself that will reinforce your desire to change. For instance, you could start with $2 worth of quarters in a jar, and every time you find yourself doing one of the things you wish to change, you take a quarter from the jar. When you go for an entire day without removing a single quarter, put another quarter into the jar. When you reach a certain amount of money, perhaps $10, you get to take the money to do something special with it, such as going to a movie or taking a friend to lunch.

Staying in Touch

Although some relationships can thrive with minimal contact, most benefit from ongoing contact. For example, after years of dealing with a serious illness, my mother learned the value of support. She came to realize that her lack of close connection with others—being Mom to five children seemed to take all of her time and energies—was at least partially responsible for her years of debilitating depression. She became very adept at staying in close touch with her family and a wide circle of friends and acquaintances. Some of her strategies included sending note and post cards with even just a few words of friendship or encouragement, regular letter writing, phone calls (occasional to frequent depending on the friend), regular visits, shared activities, doing favors for people with special needs like taking friends along when she went shopping and buying them special treats. She loved to pick blueberries and spent many summer afternoons in the blueberry fields, picking many more blueberries than she could use. She then delivered them to her friends. The berries were always a welcome gift. Much of her attention was focused on maintaining her support. Her gentle, loving care was reciprocated. Her life became rich and full.

There is now a new way of staying in touch with others: email. Computers have become much more widely available and their use has been simplified, making email available to more and more people. Anything from brief messages to lengthy letters are acceptable in this informal format (depending on your correspondent).

Commitment

You may find that regular, scheduled contact is the best way to assure staying in close connection. It means making a commitment to the friendship. For instance, one woman in the Study said that she had lost track of a good friend for several years. They met again when grocery shopping, and both exclaimed how much they had missed the other. They arranged to meet for lunch. At that reunion lunch, they decided each time they lunched together, they would set up the next time to meet so they would always have a lunch date scheduled. Sometimes they had to reschedule, but that was acceptable. This scheduling assured that they maintained their close connection. Their friendship has now flourished for many years.

Another woman told how she has a regular date with a friend on the same night of every week. Others have group meetings on the same day each month, for example the third Tuesday. When something comes up and such a commitment doesn't work on a particular occasion, you can reschedule or just look forward to the next time.

Friends are likely to feel honored if you let them know that you are committed to them. Commitment can mean things as simple as remembering their birthdays, having regular time together, remembering something they tell you that they need support with, or just keeping in touch.

This passage from *The Little Prince* (Saint-Exupéry, 1943) describes the importance of commitment in friendship. When the little prince meets the fox, he tells fox that he is looking for friends, and the fox tells the little prince how to "tame" him:

"You must be very patient," said the fox. "First you will sit down at a little distance from me—like that—in the grass. I shall look at you out of the corner of my eye, and you will say nothing. Words are the source of misunderstandings. But you will sit a little closer to me, every day. . . ." The next day the little prince came back. "It would have been better to come back at the same hour," said the fox. "If, for example, you come at four o'clock in the afternoon, then at three o'clock I shall begin to be happy. I shall feel happier and happier as the hour advances. At four o'clock, I shall be worrying and jumping about. I shall show you how happy I am! But if you come at just any time, I shall never know at what hour my heart is to be ready to greet you. . . . One must observe the proper rites."

Have you stayed in touch with people from your past? If not, how has this affected you loneliness?

_____

_____

Do you feel that you need to increase your contact with some of your friends? If so, how do you plan to do this?

_____

_____

Validation

To validate someone means that you have heard what that person has said and that you understand and believe what was said. Validation can be a very powerful tool in deepening friendships and helping others to feel better about themselves or their situation. In order to validate others, you have to learn *not to interrupt, to be still and to just listen*. For instance, one man in the Study was feeling very frustrated because his boss never seemed to notice when he did a good job or put in extra time on a project. He shared his frustrations with a friend, who listened without interrupting to offer advice or share his own stories until asked. This deepened their friendship considerably and also helped the man in the Study to feel better.

Validation is especially valuable when one person has been through a very difficult time. The experience may be recent or it may be something remembered from the past. A woman in the Study spoke about finally telling a close friend about the emotional abuse she had received as a child from her classmates. Her friend's response was, "That sounds so awful. I am so sorry this happened to you. You didn't deserve it. No child deserves that kind of treatment." The woman in the Study said that talking about it, and hearing her friend's response felt as though "a big load was taken off her shoulders" and it brightened her day.

Clearly, in addition to deepening friendships, validation from others is a very effective technique for helping to relieve the effects of trauma.

Example

You meet a friend on the street. You tell the friend you have a horrible pain in your shoulder and that you are afraid you have a serious injury. You are afraid you may need surgery. You are working on an important project and are afraid you won't be able to finish it on time. There are several ways your friend could respond. Which one would feel best to you?

Your friend says, "I'm sorry you are having such a hard time, and asks, "Is there anything I can do to help?"

Your friend interrupts to tell you that things could be worse and you are lucky you didn't break your leg the way he did three years ago, and he goes on to tell you about it.

Your friend says, "It doesn't sound so bad, you'll probably just get over it."

Why would that response feel best to you?

Example

You are walking with a good friend. She tells you that when she was married to her first husband he was very abusive to her. She describes some of the details of the abuse, and tells you how badly the abuse made her feel about herself. Which of the following responses feels best to you?

You say, "I am sorry he treated you so badly. You didn't deserve to be treated that way. I really like you."

You say, "I know a woman who was abused. I think it was her fault. Did you do something that made him so mad at you?"

You say, "That's nothing! Let me tell you what happened to me."

You say, "If you had really been abused, you wouldn't be able to hold a job and support your kids."

You say, "I don't want to hear about this. Why can't you talk about good things?"

Why did that response feel best to you?

What do these examples tell you about what you want from your friends?

What do these examples tell you about how you want to respond to your friends when they are sharing with you?

_____

_____

_____

_____

Note that there may be times when your friend tells you something that is so upsetting it makes you feel uncomfortable. It is okay for you to tell your friend that it is hard for you to listen because it makes you feel so bad and to suggest that he or she should talk to another friend or see a counselor. For instance, one woman who had been sexually abused when she was a child gets flashbacks and intrusive memories when others talk about sexual abuse. When that subject comes up, she asks that the subject be changed or the incident shared with someone else. Being a good friend does not mean you have to always be there for the other person and meet all of their needs. If you are uncomfortable, tell your friend so.

Write about a time when someone validated an experience you had.

_____

_____

_____

_____

Being a Gracious Host

Good friends often spend time in each other's homes. Making these times together special for both of you can enrich your friendship. You can make your friends feel welcome and comfortable in your home by doing the following:

- Focus your full attention on your friend.

- Turn off the television and radio when you are talking or involved in an activity together. Turn off the stereo or CD player or have only quiet music playing in the background.

- Reduce distractions by turning off your phone and letting the answering machine pick up the messages.

- Ask other family members to be friendly and welcoming but not too intrusive.

- Confine pets if they tend to jump on people, beg for attention, or are frightening.

- Avoid discussion of personal matters with family members while friends are there.

- It's always nice to pick up clutter before friends arrive. But if they arrive before you have had a chance to do that, or if they stop by unexpectedly, don't apologize and don't worry about it. Enjoy their visit.

Now, list other guidelines for being a gracious host.

_____

_____

_____

Revitalizing or Letting Go

One person in the Study said that sometimes relationships just "run out of steam." Your lives seem to go in different directions. One or the other of you develops a very consuming interest. You develop new and different friends. Your old friendship doesn't seem vital and alive. If the friendship is important to you and if you really like the other person, you can both work together to revitalize the relationship

Discuss the situation with your friend. If he or she is interested in revitalizing the relationship, work together to develop a plan for how you are going to do it. You could decide that you are going to eat lunch together regularly. Or talk on the phone one evening a week. You may want to commit to sharing a special activity like going to a play or a concert regularly. You could work together on a project of mutual interest such as developing a homeless shelter in your community.

There may be times when the friendship is not valuable enough to one or both of the people to take the time to work together on revitalizing it. If that is the case, if the commitment is not there, let it go. Refocus your attention on other activities where you will meet possible new friends.

CHAPTER 12

Developing and Sustaining an Intimate Relationship

I'm a person who is very comfortable with being alone yet loneliness has been with me at times. It seems to be connected with the desire to be with a special person sharing things together.

—A woman in her forties

Many people seem to want, and even crave, very close or intimate and trusting connections with others. However, finding such relationships and keeping them strong is often frustrating and difficult. You may be searching for a life partner, perhaps to marry, or you may be looking for friends with whom you will have very deep connections. Or you may already have a life partner and/or friends to whom you feel closely connected and yet something seems to be lacking and you wish for something more from these relationships.

In this chapter you will learn what, to you, makes up an intimate relationship. You also will learn to identify those relationships in your life that are intimate and trusting and those that are not, and you will explore how to create change in close relationships, how to enhance them, and where to meet prospective intimate friends and partners.

When discussing intimacy, one person in the Loneliness Study said, "Though I consider myself a loner, I have been living with my significant other for almost twenty years. I think the fact that I have had a sustaining friendship/partnership for so many years, has been the main reason why I have been able to work, live, and enjoy my life. Prior to establishing such a relationship, I was quite self-destructive, indulged in alcohol and abused prescription drugs. On several occasions, I attempted suicide. Now I look forward to each day, even though there have been and undoubtedly will be many hurdles ahead. I'm looking at my experiences as opportunities for learning rather than something to avoid or complain about."

What Is an Intimate Relationship?

Intimacy can be described as emotional closeness, caring, affection, trusting friendship, or simply as having a strong connection or bond with another person. Some people think that intimacy is the same as having sex or being sexually involved with someone. This is not true. You can be intimate and trusting with someone and not be sexual. For example, a relationship with a close friend with whom you share personal information and spend enjoyable time can be very intimate and totally asexual. On the other hand, you can be sexual with someone with whom you are not intimate and whom you do not trust at all. A person who becomes sexually involved with someone on a first date does not know that person well enough to be truly intimate, and does not have enough information about that person to trust him or her. You can have sexual relations with someone you do not want to be with at all and who is even hurting you.

Sex may or may not be part of an intimate relationship. In some relationships, it may not even be considered an option—such as with your best friend or a family member. At other times, when it might be considered, it is up to both you and the other person to decide whether this is what you want to do.

An intimate relationship is always *mutual* or *reciprocal*. That means that the relationship "goes both ways." Both of the people in the relationship care deeply about each other, share openly with each other, and take equal responsibility for seeing that the relationship feels good. It means talking and listening to each other. If the intimate relationship is with someone with whom you live, it may mean sharing household chores and responsibilities, and providing some care for each other when needed.

Trust and intimacy go hand in hand in relationships. If you have a trusting relationship, you have confidence in the other person and that person has confidence in you. You each have a sense of how the other person will respond, and feel comfortable that the response will be validating and affirming.

Intimate and trusting relationships don't feel good all the time. It's normal to sometimes be grumpy, out of sorts, not feeling well, or even angry and irritable. Everyone has bad days or bad times. This does not mean the relationship is no longer intimate or that you can no longer trust the other person. It just means that it is a difficult time. Such difficult times usually pass quickly. If they don't, you and the other person can talk about what you each need to do to make the relationship feel right again. In having such a discussion, it is helpful to use "I" statements such as those described in chapter 6, "Building Effective Communication Skills."

If you have been lonely for a long time, or for most or all of your life, you may have a hard time understanding what an intimate and trusting relationship is. You may feel as if you have always been surrounded by people who don't know you and treat you badly. Or you may not have anyone around at all. To understand the nature of intimacy, it helps if you can think about some person in your life with whom you had a good interaction or relationship, even if it was only for a brief time.

For instance, Don is a man in his thirties who has spent most of his life in a wheelchair due to a chronic illness. He was placed in foster care when he was very young and moved from place to place until he was old enough to have his own apartment. Most of the people in his life have been caregivers with whom he felt little connection. However, Don remembers a very special teacher he had in third grade. This teacher spent extra time with him before and after school and took him on special outings on weekends.

They talked about matters that were important to Don. When Don was with this teacher he felt "good inside," loved, and supported.

One man in the Study said, "I enjoyed a loving relationship with a very loving and caring man for about three years. It worked because we enjoyed a mutual respect, a mutual desire to help and please each other, and I was very comfortable in his genuine concern for my safety and well-being. I felt cherished for the first time in my life. He died suddenly, but I still treasure his memory and his influence."

Exercise

Write about a person in your life with whom you enjoyed an intimate and trusting relationship. It could be a spouse, family member, friend, teacher, employer, or caregiver—anyone who has had a significant positive effect on your life.

_____

_____

_____

Exercise

The following exercise will help you to learn more about identifying the relationships in your life that are intimate and trusting.

Make a list of the people with whom you interact regularly. They can be family members, friends, coworkers, or health care professionals.

Name:

1. _____

2. _____

3. _____

4. _____

5. _____

Beginning with the first name, ask yourself the following questions about your relationship with each person on your list. Consider each question carefully. If you have an intimate and trusting relationship with that person, you should be able to answer "yes" to each question (most intimate relationships may need some tweaking here or there, but in general they would meet these criteria).

1. Do we treat each other well?

2. Are we loving, deeply caring, supportive, and respectful of each other?

3. Do we avoid criticizing, judging, or blaming each other?

4. Do we listen carefully to each other?

5. Can we talk to each other about what we are working on, difficult times, personal issues, hopes, dreams, and goals?

6. Do we share fun and interesting activities with each other?

7. Do we avoid sharing personal information about each other with others?

8. Are we forgiving of each other?

9. Do we accept each other as we are and avoid trying to change each other?

10. Do I feel safe when I am with this person?

11. Do we have mutual understanding and empathy for each other?

12. Is this a loving relationship?

13. Do we work through conflict with each other by compromising and finding solutions that meet both people's needs?

14. Do we enjoy time together but also have interests as individuals, each having our own space and our own friends?

15. Can we share the "highs" and "lows" of life with each other?

16. Does the relationship feel *right*? Do you feel good about yourself, your partner (or friend), and the relationship?

17. Are statements like the following common in your relationship?
    - "I care about how you feel."
    - "Good luck at your new job; I know you'll be terrific!"
    - "I'm here for you. Let me know what you need."
    - "Let's talk about that hard time so we can work together to resolve it."

Marriage and Committed Relationships

Many people who are not married or in a committed relationship seem to crave such a relationship. If you are one of these, you may think that when you finally marry or enter a committed relationship, your loneliness will end and your life will become perfect. You may have been brought up to believe that once you are married, your life will become all roses and good times. Although it is true that many people who are married or are in a committed relationship find these relationships very satisfying, they are not a cure for loneliness or for a life that feels inadequate. Unfortunately, there is no prince on a white horse or princess with magical powers to carry you off to live happily ever after.

However, several people in the Study did say that their relationship was currently curing their loneliness in statements such as these: "Now that I have found my life partner, I no longer have a problem with loneliness." And, "The relationship I am in now is supportive and has eased or almost eliminated my loneliness."

If you are not in a committed relationship, would you like to be in one?

Why do you feel this way?

_____

_____

_____

Meeting a Prospective Partner

If you want to be in a marriage or a committed relationship, how can you meet someone who might be eligible? It seems that people have been asking this question forever. Unfortunately there is no easy answer. It happens by chance. For instance, one person in the Study said, "I went back to college . . . where I met Tom. His attention to me was an incredible surprise. From the first day we met, he accepted me for who I was and where I was at. We talked for hours and hours about everything. Math, chemistry, physics, logic, philosophy, friends, movies, school . . . we truly developed an intense friendship before anything else."

To increase the likelihood that you will connect with someone who could become your partner, you must take action. You can't stay home and wait. All of the strategies in chapter 8 on reaching out that will connect you with friends and supporters are also good ways to meet possible partners. You may want to review that chapter. Also, you may want to try some of the following strategies that have helped some people (others feel uncomfortable with them—do whatever feels right to you). Note that none of these are guaranteed to work.

Personal Ads

Write a short ad that describes your positive qualities and the kinds of activities you enjoy. Make your ad warm, upbeat, and a little sensual. Avoid negative wording. If you are looking for a person with certain qualifications (smoker or nonsmoker, use of alcohol, political persuasion, etc.) be clear about them. Keep your ad short and straightforward. Submit it for publication in a newspaper in your area or one that is of particular interest to you, or to magazines or a Web site on the Internet.

Use a mailbox service to receive responses so that you don't give your phone number to people you don't know. When meeting someone you have not met before, be sure to meet in a public place. Don't let the other person know where you live and avoid going to their home until you feel very comfortable with him or her—usually after several meetings.

Dating Services

There are many dating services available. Some of them cater to people of a certain age, sex, or background. Although each of these services is different, they all try to learn about you, and then connect you with someone whom they think would be a good match for you. Some services check people's references before accepting them as clients and some don't. As with personal ads, meet the person for the first few times in a public place such as a restaurant or cafe.

Enlist the Help of Friends

Your friends know you well. Because of that, they often can be of great help in introducing you to prospective partners.

Avoid restricting your options. You may be looking for a tall, slim, bookish man and meet someone who is short, stocky, and loves sports, but who may become your life partner. Be open to those from other ethnic backgrounds, races, and even those of widely different ages.

You will have a hard time finding a partner if you:

- Are desperate to find somebody. One woman said she finally found someone only when she stopped looking.

- Come across as too needy and "clingy." The other person may feel claustrophobic and hit the road.

- Expect the relationship to be successful quickly. Give yourself plenty of time to get to know the other person before becoming too intimate.

- Compare each person you meet with some ideal from the past, such as your high school sweetheart.

- Believe that all the good prospective partners are already taken.

It's up to you to decide with whom you want to be in an intimate relationship. Others may try to influence your choice. Listen to your own heart.

Taking Care of Your Relationship

As with any successful undertaking, a successful committed relationship requires time and attention. If you don't give a relationship the time and attention it needs (and continue to pay attention to your own needs), you may find that being married isn't all it's cracked up to be.

One person at a focus group who had interviewed a number of people about marriage and loneliness for a newspaper column said that many people had told her that "married people are the loneliest people of all."

Whether this observation is a valid statistic or just an anecdote, it does leads to this question, "Why does this come up so often?" Without further study, we can't know for sure whether married people are in fact "the loneliest people of all." But it is important to ask why so many married people are so lonely.

Perhaps the loneliness arises because of raised expectations—the belief that once you are married, everything will be wonderful and you will never be lonely again. When you marry, you may even stop making connections with others, becoming totally dependent on the marriage to meet your needs for connection. It may be because when you marry, you tend to have fewer relationships outside of marriage. If you have children, you have even less time to work on developing relationships with others and keeping them strong.

Several people in the Study felt that marriage is restrictive in that people stay in marriages even if they don't meet all of their needs for connection and support. Although this is increasingly *not* the case, people do tend to stay in marriages, even when they are "dry" or unsatisfying. You don't leave a marriage as easily as you can leave a job or a house.

Sometimes you end up playing roles in a marriage that don't express your whole self. You get really focused on the day-to-day tasks and never do a deeper "check in." Without proper attention to the marriage relationship, the tasks of day-to-day living can keep you focused on the mundane without any time for building deeper emotional connections.

As stated previously, having an intimate and trusting relationship with another person takes work. Relationships need ongoing attention, just like other parts of our lives. If they don't get the attention they need and deserve, they can become less intimate and meaningful. Following are guidelines of things to do to keep your relationship healthy and strong. You may want to copy these guidelines and post them in a convenient place as an ongoing reminder.

Guidelines for Strong Relationships

- Treat your partner with kindness, dignity, compassion, and respect. Treat your partner the way you would like to be treated and expect the same.

- Treat each other as equals. If one person feels superior to the other, the relationship is not equal or mutual.

- Share openly with each other and listen closely to what is being said. Talk about what you are feeling and be respectful of the other person's feelings. Affirm and validate each other often.

- Don't make assumptions about what your partner is thinking. Ask. And don't expect your partner to know what you are thinking. Tell her or him.

- Focus on your partner's special qualities—those wonderful unique attributes that everyone has.

- Compliment each other often. Look for reasons to compliment your partner.

- Avoid sharing personal information about your partner with others.

- Accept your partner as he or she is. Don't try and make your partner change.

- Check with your partner first before making commitments for your partner's time. For instance, if a friend asks both of you to go out to dinner, ask your partner before saying yes. Ask your partner before inviting anyone to spend time in your home. He or she may have been expecting a quiet, peaceful time.

- Keep humor and fun in your relationship—laugh and play together as much as possible.

- Practice forgiveness. Everyone does things they wish they hadn't. No one is perfect. Don't let hard feelings linger.

- Avoid references to old stuff. Appreciate your partner's growth and the positive changes you have made together in your relationship.

- Touch, hug, kiss, caress—whatever feels right. Lots of physical contact strengthens relationships.

- Be committed to the relationship, no matter what kind it is. For a relationship to work you have to be invested in it and that takes commitment.

- Compromise. When two people are in a relationship, it's not possible to always do things just the way you want them done. You both may have to make adjustments to what you want and need in order to maintain a strong bond.

- Resolve issues through discussion and compromise rather than fighting.

- When working together to resolve issues, avoid using physical gestures like shaking your finger in an accusing way or crossing your arms defiantly. Such body language will only make further discussion more difficult.

- Don't become embroiled in battles over things that don't really matter like a little dried food missed on a plate after a partner has done the dishes, or someone keeping their own space in a state of disarray. Avoid getting "bent out of shape" over petty problems. It's not worth it. Constant quarreling makes everyone feel bad. Lots of little fights can destroy relationships.

- Know yourself well. If you are feeling irritated with your partner, does it really have to do with something going on in your life? For instance, are you depressed or starting to get depressed, stressed about something, overtired, eating too much junk food or drinking too much coffee, or worried? Perhaps you need to see a health care professional.

- Each person in the relationship needs to take good care of him or herself. That means you have to do all the necessary things to keep yourself healthy and well. If one person does not take good care, the other person may have to take up the slack, causing resentment and bitterness. Make sure you eat well, exercise, get good health care, pay attention to your personal hygiene needs, spend some time each day doing something your enjoy, and stay in close touch with other friends and supporters.

- If things are changing in your lives, such as moving, changing jobs, having a child, being visited by stepchildren, parents, or other family members or having them come to live with you, having financial problems, or dealing with an illness or surgery, you will need to pay special attention to your relationship. Talk openly with each other about how you are feeling, be affectionate, and make time to do special things together.

- When working together to solve problems, state the problem, describe your feelings and state what it is that you want. For instance, if your partner is often late for dinner on the nights when you cook, you could say, "You are often late when it is my turn to cook dinner. This makes me feel upset and unappreciated. I would like you to come home on time when I am cooking dinner or to call me a couple of hours in advance if you are going to be late." If your partner agrees, fine. If necessary, you could say, "The next time this happens, I am going to eat on time so I can do the other things I plan to do, and you can warm up your own dinner when you get home." You could let your partner know that you understand that it may be hard for her or him to get away from work sometimes, but that this is very important to you.

- If you are having a hard time in your relationship and you can't figure out what to do about it, get help. See a good counselor. Sometimes there are difficult issues, such as low self-esteem, having experienced child abuse, grief, and addictions that can make relationship problems hard to resolve alone. In many cases it's best if both of you go to a counselor, but if that's not possible one or the other of you should go. Alternatively, you might want to see a counselor alone to work out some of your concerns before bringing them up with your partner.

Do any of the these guidelines ring a bell for you, letting you know that this is something you need to work on in your relationship? If so, which ones?

_____

_____

_____

Now, write any other guidelines that you feel would be helpful in your relationship.

_____

_____

_____

Working on any of these issues takes time and effort. If you feel that one or several of these guidelines are hard to observe, a good first step would be to talk with your partner about it and discuss how you are going to proceed. Writing about the issues and keeping a record of your progress can be very helpful. For instance, if you notice that you often become irritated with your spouse, write everything you can about it—when you get irritated most often, what seems to cause it, and so forth. Then, each time it happens, write it down. Try not getting irritated when you feel that you want to. Write about how that kind of struggle feels. Do it again and again. Keep a record of those days when you don't get irritated. Notice how that feels to you. You may want to give yourself a reward after you have avoided becoming irritated with your spouse for a certain length of time. For instance, if you haven't become unreasonably irritated with your spouse for a week, you could buy yourself a pair of special socks, a new CD, or go out to dinner.

If you are in a relationship where you feel that your partner does not observe some of these guidelines, you can take some action to try to change the situation. You can talk to your partner about the issue using an "I" statement like "I don't feel close to you because you share private information about me with others. I would like you to stop doing that so I can feel close to you." For instance, a woman in the study had always wanted to be close to her brother. However, she found it difficult because he always made fun of her weight problem in front of others. She could say to her brother, "I would like to be in a closer relationship with you, but I can't because you make fun of my weight in front of others." Then it's up to her brother to change. If he does, the relationship may improve. If he doesn't, his sister can choose to spend more time with people who are affirming and supportive and less time with her brother.

If you feel ready to try this now, how and when will you do it?

_____

_____

_____

_____

Reviewing Beliefs

When you were a child, you may have learned some things about being in a committed relationship that are neither true nor helpful. Several of these false ideas are listed below along with other ways you could learn to think about them, and affirmations. You also may be able to think of other statements that have influenced you that are not helpful or are actually harmful.

1. Relationships should just happen. I shouldn't have to do anything to make them happen.

   Affirmation: You have to take action to find a relationship, and to keep it going.

   How do you feel about this affirmation?

2. It seems so unlikely I will meet anyone because of my situation.

   Affirmation: I have many desirable qualities, which are likely to be noticed by an observant person.

   How do you feel about this affirmation?

3. Others will think badly of me if I do (fill in the blank).

   Affirmation: What others think about what you do is none of your business. You need to do what you feel is right for you.

   How do you feel about this affirmation?

4. You have to be in a relationship to keep from being lonely.

   Affirmation: Being in a relationship does not necessarily mean you will never be lonely. Enjoying time alone, feeling good about yourself, and having a strong circle of friends are better antidotes to being lonely.

   How do you feel about this affirmation?

   Now, write down other ideas that you have come to believe are true that may deserve further review along with positive affirmations.

   Belief: _____

   Affirmation: _____

   Belief: _____

   Affirmation: _____

CHAPTER 13

Families and Loneliness

My parents have never accepted me for who I really am. I long for their affection and their approval. I feel so lonely when I am with them.

—A man in his thirties

The family unit seems as though it should be a place where one would never feel lonely. Countless folk songs lead us to believe that we can always go home and be accepted without judgment—that loving arms will always be reaching out to us. This belief is reinforced by the images about families that we absorbed from our early childhood readers and was exaggerated and accentuated by the television families of Ward and June Cleaver, and Ozzie and Harriet—pictures of family bliss that were never quite in accord with reality.

When I use the word *family* I am referring to the people you grew up with, plus all the extended relationships that have attached to your primary family since then: in-laws, nieces and nephews, grandchildren, stepchildren, etc. You may have a large extended family or there may be only one or two people you think of as family. Some of these are people you live with or have lived with, and some are not. You may relate to your extended family differently than you do to the people with whom you now live. For example, a woman in the Loneliness Study said, "I can ignore a great deal of my mother's "controlling" behavior because it doesn't affect me anymore. But I have to confront my son's "harassing" behavior because I live with it daily." It is up to you to determine which parts to apply to which "family."

Family Issues

Many people in the Study said that issues such as those listed below had frustrated their efforts at feeling closely connected with their family members and prevent them from finding safe refuge within their families.

lack of understanding and acceptance • judgments • insensitivity • expectations • failure to keep confidences • teasing, sarcasm, and put-downs • nagging • lack of interest • differences in values • interference or meddling • efforts to be controlling • lack of validation • poor communication • distance • hierarchies or pecking orders • role playing • scapegoating • harassment • illness or disability • estrangement • divorce • death or other kinds of losses • neglect • abuse—physical, emotional, and/or sexual • alcoholism or the use of addictive substances

One man in the Study described his search for connection with a parent who had been diagnosed with a mental illness and alcoholism.

The loneliness I felt was extreme because I was alone in this. Mom was very ill. My other siblings were with my father in another state, and none of the adults I reached out to would help. I felt very sad and lonely, discouraged and hopeless. Though periodically I would be filled with great hope, as it seemed Mom was ready to accept help. I would schedule an appointment for us or her, etc., but always, these hopes were dashed as she changed her mind and became very sick again. She was also an alcoholic.

It's hard for anyone to give up the dream of close family connection. In spite of the many things that can interfere with close relationships within a family, people tend to crave this connection even after long years of frustration might have led them to believe that such close connection would be impossible. Long past middle age, some people report that they are still desperately trying to get the loving attention of a family member who has consistently ignored them or treated them badly.

Almost universally, people want affection, caring, and encouragement from family members. When people go *home*, whatever that word means to them, they want to feel safe and sheltered from the storms of the world. In the ideal family scenario expressed by many people, loneliness would never be an issue.

Do you wish for better or closer connection with your family, or does your family ever trigger your feelings of loneliness? If so, what do you think is getting in the way of feeling closely connected?

_____

_____

How would you like to feel when you are with your family?

_____

Describe what you would like your family interactions to be like.

_____

_____

Improving Family Relationships

Although there may not be a way to resolve your difficult family relationship, it may be worthwhile to try some strategies suggested by others for improving relationships with family members before you give up entirely. Many people have used the following strategies successfully to improve their relationships with their families, so that family members meet their needs for loving support more closely. You may want to try some of these strategies.

1. Treat family members the way you would like to be treated. Give them loving support. Listen closely to what they say to you. Avoid judging or criticizing them. Refer to the bulleted list of issues above that interfere with relationships within families, and make sure you are not practicing any of these behaviors. Ask family members what they need and want from you.

2. Keep in close touch with family members. Make phone calls, send email, write letters, and visit each other on an ongoing basis.

3. If you feel you are always receiving help from certain family members, turn the tables and do something to help them. If you feel that you are always giving to others and not receiving anything back, ask family members to give you a hand with certain tasks and projects. If most of your interactions with family members are concerned with "trying to fix things," stop doing that for a while and watch what happens. If matters improve, you may want to stop "fixing things" permanently.

4. Get to know family members well. Understand what they like and what they don't. Observe their preferences in color, taste, and activities. Know what interests them and discuss those interests with them. One person in the Loneliness Study shared a story told to her by her oldest brother. He told her he was seeing a counselor who had instructed him to get to know his mother—because at age fifty he was still furious with her for the dumb things she had done when he was young, and he was often unpleasant to her. So he began to lunch with his mother once a week or so. She was very pleased with the attention she got from this otherwise self-centered man, and they were working on healing their relationship and trying to become good friends.

5. Share as much as you can of yourself with family members. Let them know what you are doing and what you like to do. Tell them of your joys and frustrations. Invite them into your life through your openness.

6. As with many other families, members of your family may be reluctant to talk openly about family problems and issues. Lack of open and direct communication may not have been taught or encouraged in your family. You can begin the process of change by encouraging open discussion and direct communication styles.

7. Perhaps one or several family members have been responsible for planning and implementing most family gatherings and activities. Over the years they may have come to resent this responsibility. If you are not one of the peo-

ple who is responsible, try initiating and organizing a family activity. It could be as simple as a potluck dinner or a picnic at a local park. Encourage and support others in doing the same thing. Try to allocate the responsibilities for family get-togethers fairly.

8. Talk to one or more of your family members about family issues that may be disturbing you. Work with them to resolve these issues. You can facilitate this process by making specific requests regarding the changes you would like to see.

9. Set up a family meeting to discuss family issues. Tell family members what you would like from them and what you don't want. See how they feel about giving you the kind of support you want. If they don't want to give you what you want, at least you will have clarity about the situation. Having had family meetings to discuss less than critical issues can pave the way to good family decision making if and when more critical issues arise.

10. Go to a counselor, either alone or with one or more family members, to get information and advice on how to work together so that family members can be mutually loving and supportive.

11. Have friends and supporters outside of your family so you are not totally dependent on family members to relieve your loneliness.

Which of these strategies do you think will help improve your relationships with your family and help relieve your loneliness?

_____

_____

List any additional strategies that might help improve your relationships with your family.

_____

_____

Family Connections That Don't Work

It is not at all uncommon for people to give up on their relationships with their family—that is to say, it is just too hard; they are not going to try anymore. For example, you might say, "This holiday season, I am not going to visit my family." Or you might say, "I am never going to another family reunion." You may avoid one, several, or many opportunities to get together with your family or specific family members. Often, such a resolve is only temporary as they are and you try and try again to make your family act like the kind of family you want it to be—where being with them, would relieve your loneliness and you would feel loved and supported.

"Letting go" can mean letting go of a relationship forever. For instance, one young woman cut off all contact with her father who had been emotionally and sexually abusive to her when she was a young child and who continued to treat her badly as an adult. Or, it may mean letting go of your expectations of a family member or members. One woman in the Study has worked to let go of her expectation that she will ever be really understood by her elderly parents who don't understand her values and give her inappropriate gifts. However, she values their love and loyalty and forgives them more and more easily as they age.

Sometimes it is clear that family members can't give you what you want—either because they have told you they can't, or because the issues are so intense and long-standing that you feel there is no possibility of change. It may be important for your emotional and physical well-being to let go of your hopes and expectations and find other ways to have your needs met. You may decide to maintain some limited contact with family members who you feel will not change. Or, depending on the issues, you may decide to have no further contact with certain family members or even with all of your family.

Who are you are going to limit your contact with?

_____

Who are you going to end your contact with?

_____

In spite of your resolve, it may be very difficult to stop or limit contact with family members. You may long for a sense of family, especially at holiday times, even if it is unrealistic. You may feel dependent upon someone you know you'd be better off avoiding, or you may be financially dependent.

Furthermore, you may have learned some thought patterns earlier in your life that make it difficult to protect yourself from abusive family members. When you were a child and unable to assess what you were being taught, you may have absorbed inaccurate or untrue ideas about the necessity to stay in touch with certain family members. It may be useful to consider these ideas now and test their validity. Or you might respond to them in a different way now—a way that would feel better to you or be in your best interests. Some of these kinds of ideas were described by the people in the Loneliness Study. They are listed below along with new ways to think about them. You may have others.

- **A sense of obligation**. On reconsideration, you could decide now that it's up to you to define what is an obligation and what is not. You don't have any obligation to see people you don't want to see. You don't have any obligation to see those who have hurt you or forced you to do things you didn't want to do.

- **You can't stay away from her or him because he or she is your _____ (father, mother, brother, sister, aunt, uncle, cousin, or grandparent).** Now you can now decide to avoid anyone you want to avoid. You don't have to spend time with people just because you are related to them. You never need to spend time with people who treat you badly.

- **You should just forgive and forget any bad treatment you received from your family members**. Instead you could say to yourself, "I need to heal from the bad things that have happened to me. I don't need to forgive anyone. I'm not ready to forgive, and forgetting is impossible."

- **You can't survive without them. They are the only family you have**. Now you can decide you can do anything you need to do to take care of yourself and support yourself. You can even create a new family for yourself.

- **You just want the whole family to be together**. Now you can decide that getting the whole family together may be a very bad idea. You can arrange to spend time only with those people who treat you well.

- **You must not hurt (name of family member)'s feelings**. Now you can decide that you need to take better care of yourself and if that means you have to hurt someone else's feelings, then you may need to do that.

- **You can't stand up to (_____ name family member) or set limits for family members**. Now you can decide you can do anything you need to do to take care of and protect yourself and others you care about, and that you can set limits for family members.

- **If a family member threatens you or treats you or those you love badly, you have to do what they want you to do or just put up with the bad treatment**. Now you can decide that if a family member threatens you or treats you or those you love badly, you have the right to do anything you need to do to get protection for yourself and those you love.

Can you think of any other thought patterns that are keeping you from limiting or ending your connection with certain family members. If so, write them here along with how you could change that thought pattern so that it more accurately reflects your current circumstances.

Old thought: _____

New way of thinking: _____

Old thought: _____

New way of thinking: _____

These learned ways of thinking are often hard to "unlearn" because you learned them from those who were responsible for your care when you were young, and because they were reinforced every day. It takes time, creativity, and persistence to change these thought patterns to reflect your current thinking. You will discover many ways to reinforce your new self-affirming positive responses and, as you do that, you will notice that you are better able to avoid family members who treat you badly and focus your attention on those who treat you well.

Some of the ways that others have used to successfully challenged their old thought patterns include the following methods:

- Write your positive, self-affirming responses on a piece of paper you carry with you and then read them over and over every time you have a few extra minutes, like while you are waiting for the bus.

- Repeat the positive responses over and over every time you notice that you are thinking about these thought patterns.

- Repeat your positive responses five times when you first get up in the morning and five times before you go to sleep at night.

- Write your positive responses over and over using different styles of handwriting, using your right hand for some and your left for others.

- Write in your journal about your positive responses.

- Make signs of your positive, self-affirming responses, hang them where you will see them often, and read them every time you see them.

Allow yourself some time to grieve and let go of your old thought patterns, maybe by doing a ritual such as burning something that symbolizes the letting go—perhaps a photo or a gift the person you are letting go gave to you.

Focus on a new goal that inspires and nurtures you, to fill the space left by the ending of the relationship.

Setting Up a New Family for Yourself

If you have become completely discouraged with trying to improve your relationships with your family, you can create a new family for yourself. This might be a good thing to do as part of making a commitment to spend time with people who treat you well.

You can set up a new family—a family of choice—by asking people you know, like, and trust if they would be willing to fill certain family roles for you. For instance, if you know an older woman who treats you as you wish your mother had treated you, you could ask her to fill that role in your life. You may think of other people to act as stand-ins for your father, siblings, aunts, uncles, and even children.

For example, one woman in the Loneliness Study had tried for many years to heal her relationship with her family, but in spite of all her efforts, they continued to be emotionally abusive. Finally, she decided she had had enough. She broke off all contact with them. She stopped going to their homes for family gatherings and refused to talk to them on the phone. She then asked her neighbors, an older couple with no children with whom she already had a warm relationship, if they would be her "new" parents.

They were delighted to accept her invitation to play that role in her life. Now they talk often, share fun activities, and spend holidays together. You may not feel ready to do this now. However, you can keep this option in the back of your mind and do it whenever it feels right to you.

If you would like to create a new family for yourself, who would you want in your family—mother, father, sister, aunts? If you have people in mind for these roles, write their names below beside the role. If you don't have any people in your life right now who might be able to play these roles, write their names in whenever you find such a person.

Family Role	Person

Creating a Supportive Family

If you are a parent whose children are still living with you, you have the opportunity to take some actions now, while they are growing up, that will help them to feel closely connected to you and other members of the family throughout their lives. You can prevent loneliness from becoming an issue for them. The following parenting guidelines will help. You can copy these guidelines and post them in a convenient place.

Guidelines for Parents: Do's and Don'ts

Do's

- Always treat your children with dignity, compassion, and respect. Do not allow anyone else to treat your children badly.

- Give your children plenty of positive attention—focus on their positive qualities.

- Involve your children in making family decisions and solving problems. Hold regular family meetings that include all the members of the family.

- Spend lots of quality family time doing fun things together—playing games, reading stories, going on hikes or bike trips, visiting museums, working on projects.

- Eat meals together without television—so you can focus your attention on each other—avoid fighting at meals, discuss issues of mutual interest, and be sure everyone has a chance to share their thoughts.

- Limit the amount of television viewing and computer use to allow for more positive family interaction.

- Make birthdays a very special celebration of the life of your children—let them know clearly what very special human beings they are and how much you love and cherish them.

- Assist children in getting to know extended family members who treat them well.

- Reward your children with positive affirmations for treating each other nicely.

- Listen closely to what your children say. Encourage them to share with you their experiences, thoughts, and feelings openly and without fear of retribution. Share your experiences, thoughts, and feelings with them.

- Let your children be who they want to be.

- Encourage your children to appreciate diversity. Teach them to treat others with kindness and respect, to understand that all people are equal and deserve to be treated well in spite of differences in physical appearance, racial, religious, or ethnic background, gender, sexual preference, intelligence, or disability.

- Encourage your children to bring their friends home to play and spend time with your family. Make your home a safe and happy refuge for your children.

- Be a role model for your children by treating others well.

Don'ts

- Abuse your children in anyway—physically (inflicting pain on the child's body), emotionally (name calling, teasing, put-downs, sarcasm, taunts, threats, ridicule) or sexually (sexual abuse of any kind, including inappropriate viewing or touching, sexual innuendoes, and teasing about body changes).

- Inflict harsh, demeaning, or abusive punishments.

- Nag about things that don't matter—save your "fire" for the big things like drugs and alcohol.

- Bicker or fight with your partner—resolve disputes by discussing the issues until you reach a resolution.

- Set up unreal expectations for your children—such as expecting that a child who enjoys farming and working with animals will become a senator. Support them in their interests and decisions to do what they want to do with their lives.

- Blame and/or shame them.

- Engage in behavior that might be frightening or dangerous to your children. If you or any other family member uses alcohol, or illegal drugs, or engages in violence—you must protect your children from that behavior. The person responsible for the children's welfare should seek help or leave the home until the abusive behavior is under control. If you are in the position of protecting your children from an abusive family member, see a counselor right away for support and recommendations. If you don't have a counselor, call your local mental health agency or child protective services.

Write any other guidelines you can think of that would help to ensure that your family will stay closely connected and that family members will be an ongoing source of loving support for each other.

_____

_____

Now, write any of the guidelines that are *not* being followed in your family and what you can do to change that situation.

Guideline that is not being followed:

_____

What you are going to do to change the situation or circumstances:

_____

_____

_____

Guideline that is not being followed

_____

What you are going to do to change the situation or circumstances:

_____

_____

_____

CHAPTER **14**

Living Space, Community, and Loneliness

Community gives you a sense of belonging relative to space.

—A man in his seventies

What Is Community?

Being part of a community helps many people to feel connected to each other and relieves feelings of loneliness. What is community? How does one define community? *The American Heritage Dictionary of the English Language* (1992) describes community in several different ways. One is as a group of people living in the same locality and under the same government. For most of us, though, community means a lot more than that. It more closely matches the definition that includes the words *similarity, identity, sharing, participation*, and *fellowship*. A person in the Loneliness Study said, "The health of a community can be gauged by how connected or disconnected from others the people in the community feel."

What does the word *community* mean to you?

_____

_____

_____

You may be a part of several different communities. For instance, you may be part of a church community, or a community of those who live in a small area, such as ten families who live on an island. You may be part of a larger community, which is your town, or a part of the community where you work. You may be part of a women's community, or an ethnic community in a large city. The world is the biggest community of all—it is sometimes referred to as the international community.

One woman in the Loneliness Study lives in a household with five other women. They consider themselves a small community. They also feel that they are part of the town community in which they live. A group of people working together to resolve an economic justice problem consider themselves a community. Another group of people who live near each other in a rural area meet for dinner one night a week. They call these dinners "community dinners." You may feel that a gathering of people who meet to dance Western swing together is a Western swing dance community. You may even feel that your extended family is a community.

For instance, I live in a small rural town. I feel a sense of community here because there is a mutual concern for each other, we have similar lifestyles, and we are supportive of each other in difficult times. We also share occasional social activities and work together on community projects such as an annual apple pie festival.

What are some feeling words that you can connect with being part of a community?

Name some of the communities that you feel part of or connected to:

Write the name of the communities with which you have the strongest connection, why you feel that connection is strong, and what you want to look for in communities with which you become connected. For example, Beth feels strongly connected to the women in a women's group she has attended for several years. She feels the connection is strong because the other members of the group affirm and validate her and her life experiences. They make her feel good about herself. She knows that if she ever needs help, she can call one or several of the women in the group for support. When she assessed the value this community has for her, she realized how important affirmation and validation are for her, and as she gets involved with other communities she will look for that kind of affirmation and validation. .

Write the name of a community with which you have a strong connection:

Why do you feel that connection is strong?

Write the name of another community with which you have a strong connection:

_____

Why do you feel that connection is strong?

_____

_____

What have you learned from assessing these connections that will help you to assess new communities of people with which you might become connected to relieve your loneliness?

_____

_____

It may be that you feel your life is very restricted—that you don't have close connections with communities of people who might help to relieve your loneliness. For some people this is not a problem. They like to be alone and don't care about not feeling part of a community.

Do you wish you had more of a sense of community in your life? If so, why?

_____

_____

Perhaps you move frequently and have not been able to put down the kind of roots that help you to find your "natural" community. Or you may live in a rural or isolated area, an unsafe or unfriendly urban or suburban area, or have responsibilities at home that keep you from getting out, or you may lack transportation. You may be homeless. In the following sections, you will take a closer look at these problems and see some ideas on resolving them. If your specific problem is not discussed, perhaps some of these ideas will help you to use your own resources to find solutions that will work for you.

Moving Often

One woman in her sixties wanted a life change to reinvigorate herself. She felt it was time to "shake things up" and move on. So she moved to a totally new area where she knew no one and built herself a new life. Most of us would not have the courage to make such a move. Most of us find the prospect of moving to a new community daunting at best. One man in the Study said: "When I was seventeen, I moved from a rural community to a major city. I experienced what I later learned is called 'culture shock.' I felt isolated, out of place, anonymous. I had difficulty meeting new people. Where I used to live, we all knew each other. There was no need to 'prove' oneself."

Another woman described how she married and moved from California to live with her new husband in Vermont. In Vermont she had no friends and was physically isolated living in a rural area. She also found that cautious New Englanders were friendly but slow to accept her. Her shyness added to the problem. She says it took about two to four years as she slowly unpacked her boxes and joined classes and dance groups, to come to know others in her area with whom she could connect. Eventually, she found friends who were willing to interact and share more deeply. During this process she became more self-confident and outgoing. But it took persistence and time. Now she says she doesn't get lonely anymore.

When you move to a new area where you have no connections, you have to work at building a network of people with whom you feel comfortable—to create a sense of community for yourself. It takes energy and action. Sometimes it's hard to find that energy after the huge energy drain of moving. You may want to take some time off, just settle into your new space, and be with your loneliness until you recover from the move. When you are ready to go out and meet people, the following ideas might help you. Check off those that you think might be helpful to you.

_____ Go to places where people who have common interests congregate. Or go to places where there will be people around your age or those with similar backgrounds. Spend more time in those places where you feel most comfortable.

_____ Visit several churches in your new neighborhood, get involved in the church that feels best to you.

_____ Attend meetings of clubs and support groups in your new area. Join those that feel right to you.

_____ Take a class in some subject you find interesting.

_____ Ask colleagues at work for ideas on places you could meet possible new friends.

When you move often, the process of building new connections each time you move can become very tiring. Think about those strategies that worked well for you in the past and use them again to build new connections in new locales.

Write a strategy you used in a previous move that worked well that you could use again:

_____

_____

_____

If, when you move, you think that you won't have to make new friends because people from your old hometown will come to visit you, think again. A more practical view would be that it is often best to try to make new friends, and be grateful when old friends come to visit.

Living in a Rural or Isolated Area

Many people who live in rural areas are very lonely. This is a difficult problem to solve because of the following reasons:

- There is a lack of public transportation.

- There are long distances to go to be with others or have others be with you.

- There are very few community events.

- There is no neighborhood.

You may always feel somewhat lonely if you live in a very rural or isolated area. If this is very troubling, you may want to consider moving. If you don't want to do that, or moving is not an option, you will probably have to use a combination of several different strategies to relieve your loneliness. If you live in a rural area, which of the following ideas might help you to relieve your loneliness? Check off those that you think might be helpful to you.

_____ Work on being very comfortable spending time alone. See chapter 4, "Enjoying Time Alone."

_____ Take advantage of every opportunity to get to places where you know people will be.

_____ Keep up your correspondence with friends and family members. Respond to letters in a timely fashion so you will hear back more often. Don't always wait for people to write back to you before writing again. Write to them when you feel like it, or when you have something to share.

_____ Make good use of your phone—if you can afford it—to talk to friends and family members who can help to relieve your loneliness. If your phone budget is limited, save your phone use for these times. Make use of the mail, which is much cheaper, to make business connections, such as placing orders.

_____ Get connected to the Internet. Join chat groups with people who have interests similar to yours and with whom you can share support. For more information on using the Internet to relieve loneliness, see chapter 3, "Relieving Loneliness."

List any other ideas you think might help you to feel less lonely, even though you live in a remote rural area.

_____

_____

Living in an Unsafe or Unfriendly Urban or Suburban Area

If you live in an unsafe or unfriendly urban or suburban area, you may be afraid to venture out. Of course, the best solution to this problem would be to move to an area where you do feel safe. However, this may not be possible or financially feasible for you at this time. It may be a long-term goal—one that you can start working on now. But what can you do in the meantime to relieve your loneliness? Check off the ideas that you think might work for you.

_____ Keep your eyes open for one or several safe people in your neighborhood —people who are your sex, age, or have some other identifying feature that makes them feel safe to you and take advantage of opportunities to connect. Then, strengthen and enhance the relationships if they feel right.

_____ If you live with others, ask them to accompany you when you go out. Perhaps one or several of those could accompany you to public transportation that will take you out of the area to places where you will feel safe.

_____ Use a taxi service that will come to your door to take you to safe places to meet others outside of your area—perhaps to a support group or a special interest group.

_____ Keep close connections with friends and family members who live in other places—call them often, go to visit them whenever you get a chance.

_____ Volunteer to work for an agency that provides daily phone check-ins with the elderly and/or disabled. You will get a list of people to call each day to see if they are okay. They will appreciate having someone to talk to—and you will feel less lonely. Build these telephone connections by listening closely to what the other person is saying, and by sharing some of your own experiences.

These ideas may have helped you think of other ideas you might use to relieve your loneliness, even though you live in an unfriendly or unsafe area. If so, write those ideas in the space provided below.

_____

_____

_____

Lack of Transportation

Many people cite lack of transportation as a cause of their loneliness. Not owning a vehicle, being unable to drive, and not having other transportation options can be formidable obstacles in the path of relieving loneliness. Perhaps one or several of the following options might work for you.

_____ Get to know the area where you live very well. Discover any resources for connecting with other people that might exist within easy walking distance for you, or opportunities for others to come to where you live easily. For instance, you could invite one or more neighbors into your home for tea, or to watch a video. Or you could host a meeting of a church group or political action group.

_____ Check out public transportation options. Are there any that you have overlooked?

_____ Ask other family members, friends, and neighbors to let you know when they are going places where you might ride along—where the destinations will give you access to opportunities to be with people you already know or the opportunity to make some new connections.

_____ Learn to drive and get yourself a vehicle.

_____ Use a bike to get to places where you can connect with others.

List any other ideas you think might help you develop connections with others, even though your access to transportation is limited.

_____

_____

Responsibilities That Keep You from Getting Out

You may have responsibilities at home that keep you from getting out and connecting with others. These same responsibilities sometimes make it difficult for others to visit you. They include having small children, elderly or infirm relatives, or a family member with a psychiatric illness.

One woman in the Study said, "The loneliest time of my life was when I was raising my five children. My husband was busy and preoccupied with his work." If you have small children and it is difficult for you to connect with others, consider some of the following options for addressing this situation:

_____ Join a play group where the children play while the parents socialize. If one doesn't exist in your area you could set one up.

_____ Ask your partner or another family member to take responsibility for child care occasionally so that you get some time away to visit with friends or to attend a meeting or group.

_____ Ask another parent to watch your child or children while you get out. Then you watch their child or children, giving them a chance to get out as well.

_____ Take your children to age-appropriate activities and events in the community, events like puppet shows, swimming lessons, nature programs, church school, or story hours at the library. Take advantage of these opportunities to meet and develop friendships with other parents.

_____ Hire a baby-sitter on a regular basis if you can afford it.

Some groups of people who became frustrated with having no time for friends, particularly parents with young children, invented an innovative way of living that gives them the benefit of always having friends close by and a strong sense of community. It is called co-housing. A co-housing group consisting of several families purchases a piece of land and builds a structure or several structures in close proximity to each other, with private space for families and communal space for group activities. The group agrees on sharing responsibilities. Sometimes they share child care, communal meals, or a communal garden. People who live this way say that it's like having one huge extended family.

If you are caretaking elderly or ill family members, then breaks to rejuvenate yourself and refreshing connections with others are a very important part of self-care. Without "time off" to get support from others and to relieve your loneliness, you may compromise your own health and well-being. You may feel as if you are the only one who can provide your loved one with good care. But it is to your advantage to let go of that idea and let others take over for you for a while. It will benefit everyone involved.

Some of the following ideas might help you to get the help you need in order to get out.

_____ Call the home health agency in your area to see if there is someone who could come into your home and provide care for your relative on a regular basis. If there is a charge for this service, see if it is covered by insurance.

_____ Check with a local volunteer agency to see if there are any programs that will provide a volunteer to come into your home and take over your responsibilities from time to time.

_____ Your local social service agency could tell you if there are any day programs that your family member could attend while you get some time off.

_____ Ask family members and friends to take over your responsibilities to allow you time off. Don't feel you have to do it all alone.

List any other things you could do that would allow you to get some time off from your responsibilities so that you can spend time with friends and make new connections.

_____

_____

Homelessness

The number of homeless people continues to grow as, in my view, our governmental bodies and society in general shirk their responsibility to those who are experiencing extremely hard times. Homelessness can be caused by any number of difficult life circumstances that may include all kinds of illnesses, disability, divorce, family friction, domestic abuse, lack of employment, fire, natural disasters, and poverty. Many families with small children are trying to get by living in unacceptable circumstances such as condemned buildings without water or power or in abandoned cars. It is important to remember that anyone's life circumstance can change abruptly, and anyone can find himself or herself without a place to call home.

How does this national problem, which is felt most acutely in large cities, have anything to do with loneliness?

1. People who live on the streets have developed some remarkable strengths to get through such hard times, strengths they can use to relieve loneliness and from which everyone can learn.

2. People who lack housing and who must live on the streets can be and usually are very, very lonely.

One doctor, with a practice in Harlem in New York City, who is trying to address the medical and mental health needs of the large population of homeless people in his area said that our tendency is to look at people's deficits. He feels that we need to focus on their strengths, and people who live on the streets have developed some amazing strengths—strengths, they need to survive in what is often a very hostile environment.

Why do you need to recognize your strengths if you live on the streets and want to relieve your loneliness? Knowing your strengths helps you to feel better about yourself, and raises your self-esteem. If you feel good about yourself as a person it is easier to reach out to others. What are your strengths?

- **Resourcefulness**. If you are living on the streets, you have to be resourceful. Your survival depends on it. You have to figure out where you are going to get your next meal, where you are going to sleep, and how you are going to keep yourself warm. You have probably become very good at this. You can use this resourcefulness to figure out how you can make and keep friends. If one thing doesn't work out for you, you will find another way to approach the situation.

- **Creativity**. You have found many unusual and unique ways to solve problems. The kind of problems most people never have to face. You are creative. This creativity can be helpful to you in finding ways to deal with your loneliness. You will have ideas that others may not think of.

- **You know how to take care of yourself.** Many people who don't have to address daily issues of survival neglect themselves. They may spend lots of time taking care of others, working, or watching television. If you live on the streets you know you have to take good care of yourself to get through this very stressful time. You do the best you can to do that. People who take good care of themselves make better friends for others. They tend not to be needy and draining.

If you are homeless, what are some strengths you have that can help you relieve your loneliness?

_____

_____

_____

The following strategies on relieving loneliness were gathered from all over the country from people who have been homeless in the past or are currently experiencing homelessness. The circumstances of their homelessness vary from place to place and person to person. In some places, a separate culture of those who are homeless seems to develop. In other places, homeless people are "on their own" and don't connect with each other at all.

Services that help people who are homeless connect with each other and help them find housing and food are much better in some areas than others. In some areas these services are awful. Communities and even individuals vary in how they treat those who are homeless. In far too many situations, those who are homeless are treated badly, ostracized and stigmatized. In other places (but not enough of them), people receive compassion and support. Given these variables, hopefully some of the following ideas will be helpful to you if you are homeless.

____ Spend time in safe places where other people in similar circumstances get together like drop-in centers and shelters. Many people say they don't go to shelters because they're unsafe. Search out those that are safe and use them regularly.

____ Take advantage of any public services that would help you to connect with others.

____ Become part of a church group that makes you feel welcome.

____ Participate in events in your community. Go to parades, rallies, lectures, art shows—whatever interests you—especially those that are free.

____ Join and become an active member of a support or twelve-step recovery group.

____ Find a place to do volunteer work—such as a shelter or a soup kitchen.

____ Work to rebuild your connections with your family. See chapter 13, "Families and Loneliness."

____ Spend time with people who treat you well. Avoid people who treat you badly.

List any other ideas you think might help you relieve your loneliness even though you are homeless.

_____

_____

_____

Other Issues Related to Where You Live

When you read about developing a sense of community and feeling connected to others, perhaps you thought of some issues that are uniquely yours that make it hard for you to relieve your loneliness—issues related to your living situation. While you read through this chapter, you may have thought of some strategies for relieving these issues. You can record your issues and the strategies you plan to use in the following forms.

Issue: _____

Ideas on how to resolve this situation. When I plan to begin:_____

_____

_____

_____

Issue: _____

Ideas on how to resolve this situation. When I plan to begin:_____

_____

_____

_____

Issue: _____

Ideas on how to resolve this situation. When I plan to begin:_____

_____

_____

_____

CHAPTER 15

The Challenges of Loneliness

It felt like it was too much for me, like there was no way I could deal with this situation, nothing I could do to relieve my loneliness.

—A single man in his thirties

There are life circumstances that may be a significant contributor to your loneliness—factors that can't be overlooked. It's easy enough to say that issues like losing a loved one, being depressed or gay or fat, or being in a wheelchair, living in poverty, or moving often do not affect your ability to connect with others, but according to the people in the Loneliness Study, this would not be true. Some life circumstances can make relieving loneliness, making connections, and even feeling good about yourself a daunting task.

Some of the most common challenges to dealing with loneliness and some ideas for resolving it are addressed in this chapter. Each challenge is different. Furthermore, your approach to addressing your situation will be unique. Your specific challenge—or set of challenges—may not even be included here. However, reviewing how others have successfully dealt with the difficulties in their lives may help you to think more creatively about how you are going to deal with your situation. There is no one solution to your problem and there may not be a solution that is an exact fit with your circumstances. Open yourself up to possibilities and see what action you can take to relieve your isolation and feelings of loneliness.

Depression

It is frequently difficult to distinguish between loneliness and depression—the feelings are so similar. Depression can keep you from reaching out to others, creating or worsening loneliness. And loneliness can make you feel more depressed. The two states create a vicious cycle. If you don't address the issue of depression, both your depression and your loneliness may worsen.

If you answer yes to most of the following questions, and you have been feeling like this for two weeks or more, depression may be causing or worsening your loneliness.

1. Are you having trouble sleeping, or are you having a hard time getting up in the morning because you want to sleep all the time?

2. Has your appetite changed—either you don't feel like eating or you feel like eating all the time, especially junk foods?

3. Have you stopped receiving pleasure from activities that you have enjoyed in the past?

4. Is your energy level low, or do you feel agitated and anxious most of the time?

5. Are you more irritable than usual?

6. Have you stopped taking care of yourself and your responsibilities, or do you have a hard time doing things that are normally not difficult for you?

7. Do you feel as if you don't care about anything?

8. Do you feel that you don't have any value, and that everything is "hopeless"?

If this simple test indicates you might be depressed, you should see your doctor for a physical examination. There are many medical causes of depression. If they go untreated, your condition may worsen. In addition, your doctor can help you decide on a treatment protocol.

There are also many simple, safe activities you can do to help relieve your depression. For example, you could do one or all of the following:

- Make sure you get plenty of light through your eyes by spending some time (at least one half hour) outdoors each day, even when it's cloudy or stormy.

- Get some exercise. Any kind of movement helps to relieve depression. Walking, running, swimming, bicycling, gardening—whatever you enjoy.

- Avoid or limit your intake of caffeine, sugar, heavily salted, fatty, and highly processed foods. Focus your diet on vegetables, fruits, and whole grains, such as whole wheat bread and brown rice.

- Do something you enjoy every day—watch a funny video, play a musical instrument, read a good book, work on an interesting project—whatever you like to do.

- Tell someone you trust how you feel—just talking about depression seems to help.

For more ideas on how you can help yourself relieve depression refer to the following books: *The Depression Workbook* (Copeland 1999); *Living Without Depression and Manic Depression* (Copeland 1994); and *Winning Against Relapse* (Copeland 1999).

If you feel depression is an issue that may be contributing to your feelings of loneliness, what are you going to do about it?

_____

_____

Holidays and the Winter Season

You may feel lonely around holiday times because you are away from family members and friends, or you have bad memories of holidays that didn't meet your expectations, and/or you may be feeling the effect of lack of light through your eyes caused by the short, dark days of winter.

For instance, one person in the Loneliness Study said, "I have strong reactions to the weather. I have been diagnosed with Seasonal Affective Disorder (SAD). The months of January, February, and part of March are the worst for me, in terms of extreme depression. When I wake up and it is sunny, everything feels different. I love the sun. And when it rains, my mood plummets, even on a daily basis. I don't know if that is loneliness or depression, but it feels the same, or similar. Empty. Disconnected. Alone in a deep way, not in the physical sense. The sun is wonderful."

Another person said: "Over the holidays I am lonely because my family is so far away. My sons and grandsons remain in Pennsylvania, my youngest daughter in Oregon, and my oldest daughter in Colorado. Phoning and writing them helps but I still have not adjusted well. I find it hard to be anywhere during the holidays. I've applied to become the visiting grandmother at a local treatment center for children. I pray that goes through."

In addition to trying out some of the ideas listed in the previous section for dealing with depression, some of the following ideas may help you deal with loneliness around the holidays and in the winter. Check off those that you think would be helpful to you.

_____ Keep a positive focus.

_____ Plan special activities with friends to brighten up the season.

_____ Stay in close connection with loved ones—by phone, email, and mail.

_____ Create personal holiday rituals that are meaningful to you.

_____ Volunteer to visit the elderly in nursing homes or small children in hospitals.

_____ Volunteer at community activities such as serving holiday meals for people who are alone or taking gifts to shut-ins.

_____ Get plenty of light—outdoors and indoors—through your eyes.

_____ Use a light box. Get information on the use of light boxes from your physician.

List some other ideas and/or share your strategy for meeting the challenge of relieving your seasonal or holiday-related loneliness.

_____

_____

Loss of a Loved One

People in the Study described their terrible feelings of loneliness after a loved one's death. Following the loss or death of a loved one, loneliness can be devastating, even overwhelming. All the people in the Study agreed that the passage of time relieves the intensity of this kind of loneliness. Although no one can ever fill the space of the lost loved one, other activities and people can divert your attention, and your feelings of loss and loneliness will diminish. One man in the Study said: "I was very lonely after my partner died (we had been inseparable for twenty years). I tried, and friends tried, to interest me in things, but I still felt lonely. My advice to people who have a loss is to wait it out and time will ease the pain and loneliness." The loneliness decreased with time, and meeting and getting together with a new partner made it vanish.

The following activities and strategies may enhance and hasten this process:

Live your life as fully as possible.

Support others who have experienced a loss.

Stay really busy and active.

Use your spiritual resources.

Get counseling.

Talk with friends and family members.

Volunteer at organizations related to the illness of your loved one.

Listen to your own needs for being with others and for solitude and honor those needs.

Get plenty of support from others.

Spend time with pets.

Express yourself creatively.

Do peer counseling (see appendix B).

Attend a grief support group.

Become active in a social, school, or religious group.

Talk to others who have had a similar experience.

List some other ideas and/or share your strategy for how you plan to meet the challenge of relieving your loneliness that is related to grief and loss.

_____

_____

Disability or Illness

The following amazing description of living with a chronic illness and disability, and relieving loneliness, was written by a woman in her fifties.

I have chronic progressive multiple sclerosis. I can use neither leg so I must be transferred from my bed to the wheelchair, to the toilet or to the shower. I have two caregivers and a wonderful husband who loves me wholly and unconditionally. I still spend much of my time in bed, alone in my house. I was asked if I am ever lonely. Because I grew up in a Catholic family with seven children, two parents, and one bathroom, loneliness was an unattainable dream. I was never alone.

But I believe that people with chronic illnesses are lonely indeed. We aren't lonely because we are unloved. We are lonely because we are unique. We differ from the presently healthy, the presently able-bodied, and the presently well. They don't understand us.

Michael was dying of cancer. His wife, Jackie, my husband, Larry, and Michael and I were good friends. As Michael's cancer progressed, he and I realized that we had something in common, something to share. Every other week for two years, I would make coffee and Michael would arrive with a bag of warm bagels. We would sit at the kitchen table, look out at our small lake and "kvetch." We would actually talk about our illnesses, our occasional pain, and our perennial fears. We talked with one another as we couldn't talk with our loved ones. We talked about the lack of dignity, the lack of independence, and the brain-dimming power of the multitude of medications we were taking. We shared our attempts to make our loved ones, family and friends, believe that we were doing fine, that we didn't mind being sick, that we were good at it.

Michael and I laughed about our attempts to keep those who loved us so from knowing that occasionally we fell or wept or felt cheated. Michael and I wanted everyone to know that we were darned good sports. Michael knew I wasn't. I knew Michael wasn't.

Michael died three years ago. I miss him. I miss me. Sometimes I'm lonely.

I was asked what I do when I experience loneliness. Through the miracle of television, I bring the world into my bedroom. I watch reruns of Northern Exposure *and* Chicago Hope *and* MASH. *I watch CNN and C-Span. I shop by television and I now have Web-TV, the friend of the technologically impaired. I read novels and news magazines and share articles with family and friends. I connect with the world through the telephone. My parents and Larry's parents are in their eighties and all are in assisted-living or extended health care facilities. We maintain a thread of communication and support that all of us value.*

I provide telephone support to persons newly diagnosed with multiple sclerosis. They have so many questions and I attempt to answer them as fully and as honestly as I can. I also provide telephone assurance to a number of persons with severe and persistent mental illnesses. Many are graduates of the Pebbles in the Pond classes taught by my husband and his colleague. They trust me and I am inspired by their courage as they continue their wellness journeys. While the nature of their disorders differs from mine, we discover we have much in common.

For the last two months, I have been making amazing progress in the battle against my most troubling MS symptoms. I have been applying patches containing a new medication twice each day. It is still experimental, but I am delighted to be one of the heralds of the anecdotal successes I am experiencing. After sixteen years of various treatments that had dubious long-term benefit, here is dramatic relief from cramping and fatigue and spasms. I can be up and out of the house and active for eight to ten hours compared with just two hours a few months ago. I have renewed HOPE! I have a new mission. My neurologist told me of another of his patients for whom this treatment has been miraculous. She and her husband came and visited me and told me of their experiences. I add my story to theirs and am eager to cautiously inform others of my advances as I get referrals from physicians and others concerned about multiple sclerosis.

And . . . perceptibly . . . the loneliness is less troublesome.

One woman in the Loneliness Study said, "There is no deeper loneliness than the loneliness you feel when you're sick and alone. You have no one to talk to. You believe that no one can help you but yourself, and you feel that you are stuck in that space forever, with no way out. It's the worst loneliness in the world." If you have an illness or a disability, you may feel as if you are in permanent exile in the world. You may feel that no one wants to connect with you because you are "different" or because your disability or illness might be inconvenient. Problems with mobility or making yourself understood can increase your feelings of isolation. If you have a visible disability or illness—a disability or illness that others can see—you may feel that people avoid you because you look different. In addition, in our society, there are still many physical and sociological barriers to full participation in activities. This increases feelings of separation and loneliness.

Some possible ideas for resolving loneliness caused by disability include the following:

- Discuss your situation with a health care professional, counselor, or member of the clergy. They may have some useful ideas on how you can relieve your loneliness given the particular circumstances of your life and those of your community.

- Explore possible services that might be available for people with disabilities in your community which would connect you with others, services such as drop-in centers, senior centers, and day treatment programs. If you are home-bound or bedridden, they may have a visitors' program. They also may have special transportation or services that would allow you to attend events or go places in the community.

- Attend a support group for people who have a disability similar to yours or a mutual social support group.

- Attend community events, activities, and groups that are of interest to you (you may need to check on accessibility in advance, depending on your need).

Are there things you could be doing that would improve your level of wellness? With some disabilities, there are things you can do to improve your general level of health, such as regular exercise, keeping up with health care appointments, and avoiding junk food. Most people tend to be more supportive of those with disabilities who take good care of themselves, and less supportive of those who don't bother to take good care of themselves.

List some other ideas and/or share your strategy for how you plan to meet the challenge of relieving your loneliness that is related to disability or illness.

_____

_____

Disfigurement

In our society, people tend to avoid others who have some kind of disfigurement. People who have unusual facial or body features or who have had an accident or disease that causes them to look different from others are often stigmatized and ostracized in much the same way as people who have a hard time learning. In some ways, life is even harder for the person who is disfigured than for the person who has a hard time learning or some other hidden difficulty, because a disfigurement is plainly visible.

Diversity programs in the schools accompanied by acceptance in the family can reduce the loneliness and isolation often felt by people who have a disfigurement or visible disability. The key factor in overcoming loneliness and isolation and the low self-esteem that so often accompanies those states is the inner strength to rise above your disfigurement or disability and "put yourself out there." *Take action.*

When others are with you, they will be able to move past seeing your disability as your most significant aspect as they come to know you. Stories abound of people who have risen to the top despite their disabilities—people like Franklin Roosevelt (former president of the United States crippled by adult-onset polio) and Steven Hawking (noted award-winning physicist and paraplegic). One person in the Study put it this way: "Some people are lonely because of their disability or disfigurement and some people are not lonely despite having a serious disability or disfigurement."

Some other ideas for relieving the loneliness caused by the isolation of disability or disfigurement include the following:

- Develop a specialty. Find something you are good at and do it. Connect with others who have the same specialty and with those who admire you and what you do. One woman who has never been able to work because of a disfigurement knits sweaters and donates them to relief programs and is a weather observer for the local radio station.

- Attend a men's or women's support group or a support group for people with issues that are similar to yours.

- Get involved in an activity where your help would be appreciated and where people would have a chance to get to know you, such as delivering plants at a hospital, waiting on people in a library, or working on a Habitat for Humanity house.

- Go to places where you know you will have a good time, even if you don't have anyone to go with—like a concert or a movie. As people see you around, they may begin to connect.

One young man said, "Avoid forcing yourself to make friends. Set up opportunities for people to get to know you and let it happen."

List some other ideas and/or share your strategy for how you plan to meet the challenge of relieving your loneliness that is related to disfigurement.

Being Older

At one focus group, a seventy-year-old man said, "I never thought I would be in this place in life. I thought I would get married one time and we would always be married. Now I have two ex-wives and I am alone. I'm too old for anyone to want to get involved with me." He said, and others agreed, that having a wide range of interests is an important asset as you retire and age. Being interested in many things gets you out of your house and provides you with a way to connect with others.

The group agreed that the experience of loneliness depends on the personality—some people feel it more acutely than others. One woman said, "I knew I didn't fit in, but it really didn't matter to me." A common philosophical thread running through this kind of stoic acceptance is reflected in this statement by a woman in her sixties who said she has been very lonely all her life and doesn't know why. "As I get older, my loneliness gets easier to bear." Some felt that as older people, they are not only more "set in their ways," they are also are "pickier" about whom they spend time with. They look for people who feel "just right."

Connections with extended family, especially adult children and grandchildren, are a wonderful source of connection for many elderly people. People who have no children are saddened that this kind of family support is not available to them—causing them to feel they have to work harder at strengthening their connections with friends, and to keep those connections strong.

Although some people bemoaned the thought of having to spend time in elderly housing or nursing homes, one optimistic woman said she was excited about the variety of options that would be available to her. Note that these options were not available in the past. They include continuing to live in your own home in your community with a part-time or full-time attendant, living in an assisted living facility, and a variety of other housing programs that accommodate people with special needs.

To avoid extreme loneliness in old age, it is clear that doing some or all of the following activities is helpful:

- Do some advance planning.

- Begin working on strategies to relieve loneliness before the situation worsens—as one *approaches* old age rather than when one is in the midst of it.

- Maintain a wide range of interests.

- Stay in close touch with friends and acquaintances from the past.

- Establish and maintain strong ties with supportive members of your extended family.

Many people spoke of the need for advance planning as one approaches retirement and the later years of life. For example, one woman had had a very active life working as a professional seamstress out of her home in an apartment in New York City. Her days had been filled with interesting people coming and going, coupled with an abundance of satisfying creative work. But as the availability of fashionable clothing from outlets around the world increased, her business fell off until it had dwindled down to nothing. She had recognized this change as it was happening and had bemoaned her fate, but she did little to fill the empty spaces left in her life. As she aged she became more and more reclusive, and she grew bitter and cantankerous. She had a frustrating and lonely old age.

How could she have changed this scenario? Well, when she saw her business shrinking as she aged, she could have begun doing some volunteer work. For example, she could have made costumes for struggling theater companies or put her energy into making toys and doll clothes for needy children. Perhaps she could have given sewing lessons or acted as an aide or consultant to fashion designers. She could have explored the city (an activity that was not an option when she was involved with her business). She could also have frequented museums and theaters.

One woman's innovative plan for dealing with loneliness and connecting with others as she enters a time in her life when she will want to stay close to home (she lives in a place where getting out in the winter is often difficult) is to, as she calls it, "mine" her neighborhood. She takes advantage of every opportunity to get to know and socialize with the people who live close to her. When a new neighbor stopped her to ask a question, she invited her in for tea. She started a conversation with a man who walks by her house each day with his dog and they have become friends. She met other people while walking or riding her bike in the area and invited those who seemed interested and interesting to her home for informal gatherings.

All of the ways to relieve loneliness mentioned in other chapters of this book are relevant to the elderly. Some of the most popular include the following. Check off those that appeal to you.

_____ Do volunteer work.

_____ Become a big brother or big sister.

_____ Join a book discussion group.

_____ Engage in church services and church activities—attend the coffee hour after church if there is one.

_____ Get involved in organizations and civic groups.

_____ Go on vacations and retreats, and to workshops and conferences.

_____ Connect with a visitors' service—either you visit someone or have a visitor visit you. (In some communities you can arrange to have a senior volunteer stop by and visit you on a regular basis, or you can arrange to visit other people of your own age.)

_____ Explore your community—visit all the museums, art galleries, public buildings, parks, etc.

_____ Check out some new interests, options you had no time to pursue when you were younger and too busy with family and/or career.

_____ Take a course at the local community college or adult high school.

_____ Work out at the local gym.

_____ Participate in activities at your senior center.

List some other ideas and/or share your strategy for how you plan to meet the challenge of relieving your loneliness that is related to being elderly.

Sexual Orientation

Although being gay or lesbian no longer carries the stigma it once did, people who are homosexual or bisexual continue to confront obstacles in connecting with others. In a society that has long defined heterosexuality as the norm, this can be a relentless challenge that can be both draining and isolating. One woman in the Study put it this way: "Being a lesbian causes a certain level of isolation, as your very existence sets you apart from the main cultural imperatives of most heterosexual society." A man in his thirties said, "For me, my sexual orientation was the most isolating aspect of my youth. It was a major contributor to my depression and loneliness. When I finally accepted my homosexuality and rejected the sin and blame associated with it, I was far more comfortable with myself and was more open to friendships and certainly to sexual/love relationships. My loneliness and depressions gradually decreased until now they are quite rare."

One woman in the Study said, "I think the actual dealing with the 'Am I or am I not?' part of 'coming out' is extremely lonely, as you don't know who to trust or what to say. And then when you are searching for a connection—either a partner or a community—it's very lonely as well. But I have actually found more friends being 'queer,' as it is such a tight group, and loads of my 'straight' friends are still very much there for me too."

An older woman said: "I've felt lonely during a number of periods in my 'queer' life. When I worked it was very lonely because I could never talk about my partner in any specific terms—like telling coworkers that my partner and I had just bought a brand new bedroom suite and it was great. So much of your life is hidden when you are in the work world. It's lonely pretending to be someone else. Gays are very isolated and lonely in the community because we can never tell it like it is. We are always showing a side that isn't who we really are in fear that we will not be accepted. An example of all this is our not being able to dance with one another at her niece's wedding. Ouch!"

How do people deal with this difficult issue? One person said, "You have to find 'up' things to do with 'up' people." Another said, "My partner and I joined a 'committed couples' group. We met once a week and discussed a topic that couldn't be discussed anywhere else. Earth-shaking topics like: How do you handle Christmas as a couple? How do you handle finances? This allowed us some place to interact with others about our day-to-day living."

Other strategies for relieving loneliness if you are gay or lesbian include the following:

Practice self-acceptance. • Be your own best friend. • Spend time with people who treat you well. • Get affirmation through gay culture books, movies, and music. • Let go of the shame and blame associated with being homosexual. • Be open about your sexual orientation and "let the chips fall where they may." • Create a strong network of homosexual friends—both friends who are homosexual and friends who are not gay. Join a support group for people who are gay or a "committed couples" support group. • Talk with others in similar circumstances who can relate to your specific dilemma. • Choose a living space in an accepting community or area. • Give people the opportunity to get to know you well—to see that you are not any different than other people. • Get involved in community activities. • Pursue interests that will get you involved with other people. (One person met many new friends by training dogs to pull carts!) • Take a class or join a special interest group such as an aerobics or dance group, a chorus, or an orchestra. • Get involved in a supportive church community. • Host gatherings of interesting and supportive people. • Recognize that family gatherings, straight romantic movies, and conversations with people who assume you are straight may trigger feelings of loneliness and isolation—use some of the ideas in chapter 3, "Relieving Loneliness," to help yourself feel better.

If these steps are very difficult for you, seek counseling with a counselor trained to address issues related to homosexuality—ask your friends for recommendations.

List some other ideas for how you plan to meet the challenge of relieving your loneliness that is related to sexual orientation issues.

_____

_____

Intellectual Differences

People who have a hard time learning and those who have high levels of intelligence both have a hard time connecting with others with whom they can have a mutual relationship.

Those who have a hard time learning are at a great disadvantage in our society. They are often stigmatized and ostracized because of their disabilities. This stigmatization and ostracism can begin at a very young age when other children become aware of individual differences in abilities. They tease and insult the slower learner, often destroying his or her self-esteem and making life miserable for that person. Unless this low self-esteem is addressed and the person is helped to understand that one's value does not depend on intellectual or academic abilities, that person may experience an entire lifetime of feeling badly about him- or herself. These feelings are often accentuated by deep feelings of loneliness.

Not too many years ago, people with intellectual disabilities were also stigmatized by teachers and others in the helping professions, as well as by their peers. Today, children in schools, school programs, and churches are being taught to appreciate diversity of all kinds. Although as a society we have a long way to go in this regard, it is encouraging that these steps are being taken. Families can support these efforts by encouraging diversity activities and promoting the acceptance of differences in the home and in the community.

If you believe that you have trouble learning and/or have intellectual differences that are causing or contributing to your feelings of loneliness, the following ideas may be helpful.

- Try doing lots of different things. Although you may have trouble learning in school, you may find that you are much better at some things than other people. Although there are many more activities to try out, some of the things you could try are these:

  play a musical instrument

  take up woodcraft, sculpting, pottery, weaving, needlework, or painting

  study auto mechanics

  learn cooking

  learn gardening

- Meet others who share your interests and might become friends by joining groups that focus on your area of interest.

- Raise your self-esteem. That will make it easier to meet people and make friends. Read chapter 5, "The Self-Esteem/Loneliness Connection," and do the suggested exercises, repeating them over and over.

- Get involved in programs at your church, synagogue, or mosque.

List some other ideas for how you plan to meet the challenge of relieving your loneliness that is related to having a hard time learning.

People who are "smart" often feel isolated and lonely, too. They say it is hard to find others with whom they can have interesting and stimulating conversations. They also say that other people sometimes assume that, because they are smart, things are usually great for them. Sometimes others are "put off" by smart people, feeling that smart people wouldn't want to be friends with them.

One man in the Loneliness Study said that he felt very isolated when he was in grammar school because of conflicting desires. On the one hand, he wanted to fit in with the other kids, and on the other, he wanted to stand out because he always knew the right answers and wanted the approval of his teachers. He said that some kids picked on him because he was "too smart." As an adult, he has had a wider range of options to choose his friends and acquaintances from than he had as a child. He has met people who have become good friends through active involvement in community and environmental groups.

A woman in the Study also shared her experience of this dilemma. She said as far back as nursery school, she had been surrounded by children who were a couple of years behind her academically. "I was reading comic books when I was three, and handling addition and subtraction in my head by the time I was five. I can still remember sitting in kindergarten through those interminable drills where the nun pointed out the letters one by one on the wall so that everyone would learn to recite the alphabet. There were no other kids in my class who could do math and read."

She says the gap widened gradually and the loneliness deepened. "It was weird, because the same people I felt were so far behind me in 'book smarts' were miles ahead of me socially. I just wasn't good at the social stuff. I buried myself in books, particularly science fiction and fantasy. I spent more time with adults than kids. At the same time, my peers voted me class president. I was confused by that. Genuinely confused. It turned out they thought I was most qualified for the job. High school was a little easier since there were more people, but a lot harder because I knew no one and was making a change from a class of twenty-six kids who had been together for nine years. My own psychological makeup, including my lack of self-esteem and weight issues, kept me from being totally comfortable around other smart people. I had only a couple of good friends in high school, and in retrospect, I didn't even let them get to know me very well. I did try to do things that interested me. I joined and later became president of the math club. I worked on the yearbook and the student newspaper. But mostly I had a goal to learn what I could while blending in with the woodwork. By the time I was at all comfortable in high school, it was time to go to college."

One person deals with this issue by "chatting" with people on the Internet. She says, "Their interests vary the same way mine do. I no longer expect to find one or two people who I will bond with and be friends with to make my loneliness go away. Some of the loneliness is still a fact of life for me. Sometimes it isn't loneliness, just a need to be alone. Sometimes I am totally comfortable alone and I need the time away."

Some ideas for meeting the challenge of relieving loneliness when you have intellectual interests include the following:

- Strike up conversations with people who enjoy the same things you do, like art, movies, music, tours of historic areas, and hikes in natural areas.

- Avoid the temptation to watch too much television because it accentuates your differences with others and makes you feel more isolated.

- Pursue and establish connections with others with whom you can have interesting conversations—work actively at this.

- Develop strong connections to a college or university community by taking courses (or teaching courses) and become involved in activities there.

- Choose a living space in a community or area where other people with academic or intellectual interests reside.

List some other ideas for how you plan to meet the challenge of relieving your loneliness that is related your intellect.

_____

_____

_____

Poverty

Almost always, economic poverty is accompanied by feelings of isolation, shame, loneliness, and rage. People who have little income are often stigmatized in our society. In addition, they feel self-conscious and isolated doing the things they need to do to survive, such as using food stamps at the checkout counter. Reaching out to others can be difficult.

- Remind yourself that you are a valuable person. Your value is not determined by your economic status.
- Attend free community events.
- Get involved in a supportive church, synagogue, or mosque community.
- Reach out to others who have limited incomes.
- Take advantage of services that might help you connect with others, such as scholarships for classes and support groups.

List some other ideas for how you plan to meet the challenge of relieving your loneliness that is related to your economic status.

_____

_____

Being Male

Many men said that they feel it is harder for them to make and keep friends than it is for women. They said things like "Men have acquaintances and women have friends" and "Men come together over action, not the sharing of feelings." One man said, "I think it is the idea of 'machismo.'" Men in our society are often discouraged from developing truly intimate relationships. Intimacy may be perceived as unmasculine. However, many men in the Study said they crave close connection, where they can share feelings as well as activities, particularly with other men.

While women often report that they are comfortable just talking and sharing, men frequently said they were more comfortable when they were "doing something" with another person, like hunting, cutting wood, playing catch, or watching a sports event. Their talk may be more focused on what they are doing or have done than on their feelings. One man said that when he is with other men, they often "joke around." He thinks that sometimes this may be just for fun, but he also suspects that such joking around is a good way to cover up feelings or discomfort.

What do men want in relationship with other men and with woman friends? One man said, "I want to be able to weep at a movie I have attended with a friend and have it be okay. I want to be able to touch and hold hands with my male friends and not have it be seen as sexual." Another man said, "I want some real friends, people with whom I feel comfortable, with whom I can share what is of interest, and who I can tell how I am feeling, whether it's good or bad. I want more *intensity* in my relationships with others. That means talking in-depth, not just about superficial feelings." An older man said, "I want a friend who likes adventures and with whom, through the relationship, I can share something special that I can't have alone."

Qualities that men want in relationships with others include the following:

- a willingness to share feelings and experiences openly

- opportunities to do things together and reflect on those matters that are of mutual interest

- gentleness

- respect

"All or Nothing" Statements

As children, many of us were taught "all or nothing" statements that lump all men together. Such statements increase the sense of alienation from others that so many men feel. Some of these statements are as follows:

Statement: "Real men don't show their feelings."
How do you feel about this statement? Write your answer below.

_____

Statement: "You have to end up with something for an activity to be of value."
How do you feel about this statement?

_____

Statement: "A good man can handle anything, no matter how difficult."
How do you feel about this statement?

_____

Statement: "Men need to rely on themselves. Relying on others is a sign of weakness."
How do you feel about this statement?

_____

Statement: "Only sissies cry."
How do you feel about this statement?

_____

Statement: "All a man wants from a woman is one thing."
How do you feel about this statement?

_____

Statement: "If you are friendly with a woman it means you want to have sex with her."
How do you feel about this statement?

_____

How do men relieve their loneliness? One man in the Study said that he had tried to relieve loneliness with alcohol and drugs. When he realized that his strategy wasn't working and that it had negative consequences that outweighed any possible benefits, he had to rebuild his life based on new activities that involved meaningful connection without abusing substances. He said he finds making connection with others to be very difficult for him because he "comes from a long line of silent males."

Another man in the Study said that he had many acquaintances he had met over the years as an active participant in many team sports and as a spectator. However, he found that these relationships tended to be very superficial and did not meet his needs for friendship and closer connection. He worked to resolve this situation by enhancing his relationship with several of these acquaintances—three men and a woman—with whom he shared mutual interests and who were more open about discussing their feelings. He invited them, sometimes individually and sometimes as a group, to dinner at his home, to go hiking, to accompany him on some longer trips, and to share other informal activities. He offered to help them out with their chores at their homes and set up regular peer counseling sessions with two of the men. He took some risks, gradually sharing with these friends his feelings about important issues in his life. When he noticed that these attempts at deepening his relationships were helping to relieve his loneliness, he increased his efforts, noticing still other people who interested him and inviting them to share activities and to play a more significant role in his life.

Where do men meet possible friends? Several men said that they have stayed in close connection with grade school, high school, and college buddies or other friends from their youth. One man said that he has tried to "reawaken" some connections that have been dormant for a long time by contacting people through the Internet. His efforts have been "guardedly" successful. If you have the time and the interest, this strategy may be worth a try. You also might try to reach out to people you met in places where you have been employed.

The places that men tend to meet possible friends and make connections with others include the following (for more ideas see chapter 8, "Reaching Out"):

- the workplace

- fraternal organizations

- sporting activities or events

- alcoholics anonymous and other twelve-step groups

- men's or co-ed support groups

- special interest groups, such as political parties or environmental activist groups

List some other ideas for how you plan to meet the challenge of relieving your loneliness that is related to being male.

_____

_____

_____

CHAPTER 16

Pulling It All Together

What I've discovered is that it takes a lot of people in my life to keep me from getting lonely. The biggest mistake I was making earlier in my life was in expecting a single friendship, or even my relationship with my partner, to solve my loneliness problems.

—Single man in his thirties

In reading this book you have explored many different aspects of loneliness, reviewed many different ways of relieving loneliness, and you may have taken some steps to help you feel less lonely and more connected to others. You may have reached out to others and interacted with others in new ways. In this chapter, you will review what you have learned and have a chance to use what you have learned to develop a plan for how you are going to relieve the loneliness in your life.

Key Points About Relieving Loneliness

As you work to relieve loneliness in your life, it helps to remember that in order to effectively resolve your issues around loneliness in your life, you have to:

- Remind yourself, perhaps over and over, that you have resources and the ability to relieve your loneliness. You are a strong person who can create positive change in your life.

- Know that no one person can meet all your needs. It's important not to be dependent on only one person. If you are only close to one or even a few people, they may be sick, away, or busy with something or someone else when you need or want someone to talk to or just to be with. One person in the Study said: "Have a lot of people in your life with whom you share some mutual interest. Relying on only one or two people puts too much pressure on everyone. Relationships need room for natural ebb and flow, and that can only happen if we have a good-sized collection of friends so we don't rely on any one person for too much. I think that even applies to your spouse."

- Remember that you are a valuable person, and that you deserve to feel less lonely and to have loving, supportive people in your life.

- Take some action—do something. You can do it as slowly or as quickly as you want. You can take small steps or big steps. But if you are lonely, and want to feel less lonely, or lonely less of the time, you must take some action. You can take action to find new friends and supporters, and/or to improve your relationships with those people who are already in your life.

- Decide for yourself what it is you want to do and how you want to do it. No one else can make decisions for you about how to relieve your loneliness, when you should do it, who you should be friends with and who you should avoid and who you should be with in a significant relationship. It's all up to you!

- Ask your supporters for what you need and want—otherwise they won't know.

- Ask your supporters what they need and want from you. Don't assume that you know what they want and need.

- Keep your relationships mutual. Make sure you listen closely to what the other person has to say and give him or her plenty of time to say it without interrupting. Then take about equal time to share whatever it is you would like to share.

- Learn to enjoy spending time alone. Those who like to spend time alone usually feel less lonely.

- Develop interests in lots of different things. It will open opportunities for connection with others and make you an interesting person who others enjoy being with.

- Become comfortable with a variety of techniques for relieving loneliness, easy-to-use skills that will help you through difficult times.

- Work on changing those things you have discovered about yourself that may make it hard for you to find and keep friends. Matters like negative thinking, communication styles that push others away, isolating behaviors, and being habitually sarcastic.

- Know that there is no room for shaming, blaming, teasing, being rude or prejudiced, or putting others down in a good relationship.

- Stay away from people who treat you badly. This may be difficult to do, but it is worth the effort.

- Understand that working to relieve loneliness and building a circle of strong supporters can take a long time and lots of effort. In fact, one woman in the Study said that she thought she would be working on this for the rest of her life. Don't give up! It's worth it and it's fun.

- Be aware that as you change and grow, and as your life changes, you will find that you will have gained some new friends and supporters, and that because of distance and the circumstances of your life or their lives, some of your old friends and supporters may not stay closely connected. These kinds of changes are normal for everyone.

Second Thoughts

How do you define loneliness now that you have read through the book?

_____

_____

How does that definition compare with your answer in chapter 2, "Loneliness in Your Life"?

_____

In chapter 2, you wrote your short and longer term goals for relieving your loneliness. Have they changed? If so, what would your goals for relieving your loneliness be now?

In one month:

_____

_____

In six months:

_____

_____

In one year:

_____

_____

In five years:

_____

_____

Most people have many acquaintances—people they see occasionally, and with whom they may talk with briefly when they see them.

Name several acquaintances:

_____

_____

_____

If you wish you had more acquaintances, how would you work toward finding them?

_____

_____

Most people have some people they know better than acquaintances—people with whom there is some deeper level of connection. They lunch with and/or share activities from time to time with these people.

Name several people like this in your life:

_____

_____

_____

If you wish you had more people in your life whom you knew better than as acquaintances, how would you work toward finding these people?

_____

_____

Most people have some family—people to whom you are related through birth or adoption, or whom you have chosen to fill that role in your life. (This list may or may not include a spouse, partner, or significant other.) List those family members to whom you feel closest:

_____

_____

_____

Are there family members that you wish you felt closer to? If so, how do you feel you could improve these relationships?

_____

_____

Do you feel you need to build a new family for yourself or add people to the family you already have? If so, how do you plan to do that?

_____

_____

Most people have a close circle of intimate friends and supporters—people with whom you have a mutual relationship, who you see or contact regularly, who you feel comfortable with and can call on when you are feeling lonely or having a hard time.

Most people agree that it is best to have five people on this list. Can you put five people on your list now?

_____

_____

_____

_____

_____

If you can't put five people on your list now, and if you feel you need or want more people on your list, how are you going to work toward finding these people?

Strategy 1. _____

Strategy 2. _____

Strategy 3. _____

Strategy 4. _____

Strategy 5. _____

Read the following list. Which of these do you want from your friends and supporters? Check off those items that apply to your needs and desires.

_____ listening

_____ sharing—good conversation

_____ interests in common

_____ respect, trust, and honesty

_____ confidentiality about personal issues

_____ to be able to tell them anything without fear of judgment, betrayal, or reprisal

_____ sharing—good times and fun activities

_____ to be accepted as you are

_____ good advice when you ask for it

_____ to be appreciated as you change and grow

_____ support in raising your self-esteem

_____ to work with you to figure out what to do in difficult situations

_____ to assist you in taking action that will help you feel better

What else would you add to this list?

_____

_____

_____

Using Your Support System

As you have read throughout this book, strong connections with others enrich your life. In fact, they probably improve your health and reduce stress. Having a strong circle of support is especially helpful when you are going through a very hard time such as having a serious, chronic, or acute illness; having had or needing major surgery; experiencing emotional symptoms like anxiety attacks or depression; having had a loss in your life; having a lot of stress like being sued; having to move or are moving; or having your marital status change. At times like these, friendly support can make all the difference.

In the prelude to this book, I spoke about my mother's illness. I said that she spent eight years in a psychiatric hospital when I was growing up. I have often thought about how her life might have been different if, instead of trying to cure her depression with hospitalization, my mother had received the support of her sisters, mother, and a few close friends. She was very close to her sisters and her mother, but at the time of her depression she was living far from them and her contact with them was infrequent—much less frequent than it had been at other times in her life.

In addition, she had little time for connections with other people outside of the family because my father worked long hours and their budget was limited. I wonder what would have happened if my mother's mother and sisters had come to stay with her. If they had talked together for hours and hours. Perhaps they could have taken her on a trip—away from family responsibilities. Or one of them could have taken over her family responsibilities for a time. I wonder what would have happened if she had had a chance to go to a women's support group one or several nights a week, if she had had some friends who could have taken turns watching the children. Might she have been spared those long years of disability?

I do know that *support* finally did pull my mother out of her depression. A volunteer came into the hospital and listened to her—as she described it, "for hours on end." Then, as she began feeling better, she started getting together with groups of patients in what we would now call a "support group." Working with other patients, she started an ongoing support group within the hospital. After she was discharged, she went back to the hospital from time to time to attend the group. Throughout the rest of her life she put a strong focus on mutual support. She kept in close touch with her friends and always found a supporter to talk to when she was having a hard time. And she never had another deep depression.

A woman in the Loneliness Study shared the following story. She said, "I knew I was in for a hard time when I learned that my husband had a very serious chronic illness that would eventually cause his death. I called my supporters and asked them to meet me for lunch at a favorite restaurant. At the lunch, I told them what I was going to need from them over the next few months and hopefully years. It included regular times to get together and talk, phone calls, and availability for assistance and support in the most difficult times." After her husband died, she often spoke of how the support of her friends helped her make it through what could have been a very lonely time. This same support team was with her later when she experienced some very disturbing events in her family and a very serious illness.

When you have a list of several supporters, you may want to get them together so they can meet (if they don't already know each other) and so you can tell them what you would like from them in difficult times. You could invite them out for lunch, to your home for a special dinner you make, for a pot luck meal where everyone brings a favorite dish, or to a gathering in the park. Or you could even talk at the end of a hike on a mountaintop.

Some people with serious illnesses or chronic conditions have developed crisis plans they give to supporters so that their supporters know what to do for them when they can't do anything for themselves, and when they may not even be able to tell others what they want or need. This kind of crisis plan allows you to stay in control of your own life even when things are out of control. It also puts supporters at ease since they have documentation that tells them what to do in difficult situations.

Any crisis plan that you develop must include a description of what you are like when you are well (in case it is shared with a health care professional who doesn't know you), and listings for the following sets of information.

1. Symptoms that would indicate that others need to take over responsibility for your care.

2. All your supporters' names, including your health care professionals, along with their roles and phone numbers.

3. Any medications and health care preparations you use and those you need to avoid.

4. Treatments that help and those you wish to avoid.

5. A plan that would allow you to stay at home or in the community even if you are very ill or having a very hard time.

6. The names and phone numbers of hospitals or other facilities where you would prefer to receive any needed treatment.

7. A list of what your supporters can do for you that would be helpful, such as watering the plants, feeding the dog, cooking you some good food, playing pleasant music for you; and a list of what they should not do.

8. Information as to when they should stop following this plan.

In Closing

In most people's lives, work on relieving loneliness tends to be an ongoing, continuous process. You may go through periods of time when you feel content—that all is well with your life. At other times, you may notice that you feel discontented, and that some or all of that discontent is related to loneliness. Then you will know it is time to do a personal assessment and decide what it is you need to do to feel better. You will need to ask yourself these questions: Has your circle of supporters dwindled? Do you need to make new friends? Is it time to work on building up your self-esteem? Can you learn to enjoy the time you spend alone more? By using your creativity, common sense, and persistence, you can meet these challenges and relieve the loneliness in your life whenever it seems necessary to do so.

Appendix A

Starting a Support Group

Perhaps you can't find a support group that you like and you want to start one of your own. It's not a difficult thing to do. Setting it up with another person makes the process easier and more fun. There are many options for groups and there is no one "right way" for a group to be. One simple way to start a support group is to invite several people you know to come to a meeting and encourage them to invite other friends as well.

My friend told me that she would like to have a support group. I shared that with another friend. We each invited several friends to a meeting at one woman's house. There were ten people at the first meeting. The group is still meeting every Monday night after ten years. The membership has changed somewhat, but at least half of the members of the group were at that first meeting. The group is usually closed, meaning that there will be no new members. However, from time to time, if the membership gets low, new members are invited into the group. The members take turns holding the meeting in their home. No refreshments are served—only herbal tea. At each meeting, the group chooses a topic that will be discussed at the next meeting—things like your personal relationship, life challenges, and values. The first meeting of the month is reserved to catch up on the details of each other's lives. Each member gets ten minutes to talk about the topic or to tell what is going on in her life without interruption from the other members. Members converse informally before or after the sharing time. If one member has a special need, extra time is spent listening to that person and giving feedback if it is wanted. The group has an agreement about confidentiality for personal information shared in the group. No judging is allowed. Feedback is offered only when a member asks for it. Group members often get together socially and reach out to each other for support in difficult times.

Answering the following questions and taking the suggested steps might be helpful in setting up your support group. Check off your answers to the questions to help yourself summarize the information.

_____ I am going to work on setting up the group by myself.

I am going to ask (who) _____

and _____ (and)

_____ to help me set

up the group. If you are going to ask one or several other people to help you set up the group, you may want to have a preliminary meeting where everyone involved answers the following questions.

_____ I am going to have a meeting of the people who are willing to help me set up this support group at (time) _____ (when) _____

(where)_____

so we can make plans about how we want to proceed.

Why do you want to start this group?_____

_____

What kind of group do you want this to be?_____

_____

What do you want this group to achieve or accomplish? _____

_____

Will the group be open to anyone or restricted to people who share certain interests or who are alike in some way, i.e., have a similar illness or condition, are single, have weight problems, or are all women?

Optional: The group will be restricted to people who _____.

_____

When a group is always open to new members, it may be more difficult to become closely connected to the other members and to share personal information than if the group places restrictions on when new people may join the group.

Will the group always be open to new members (an open group) or will it accept members until a certain number has been reached or until a certain date and then no longer be open to new members (a closed group)?

We (I) _____ want an open/closed group _____

(circle one).

Sometimes groups get so large they become hard to manage. You may want to restrict your group to a certain number of participants. If a group is so big that not everyone present gets a chance to speak and be supported, or if there are so many people in the group that people can't get to know each other well, you may want to break the group into smaller groups.

Approximately how many people do you want to have in this group? _____

If the group has too many members, would you consider breaking it up into smaller groups? ____ y ____ n

Decide when you want to meet and for how long. Many support groups meet in the evening but they can meet any time that is convenient for the members.

We (I) I want our group to meet (when) _____ for (how long) _____ .

Find a place to hold meetings. Unless you are planning to have a very small support group that will be limited to a few of your closest friends, it is not wise to hold the meetings in your home. If the group meets in your home, that makes it difficult to stay home when you don't want attend or can't go to a meeting. Libraries, churches, schools, hospitals, and health care agencies are good places to look for free space to use for support group meetings. If there is a charge for the space, you might have to ask group members to pay dues or to pay a certain amount each time they attend. Call these facilities to get information on the possible use of their space.

Which of the following are important to you in selecting a place to hold your meetings? Check off those that are important to you.

____ free

____ low-cost

____ convenient

____ easy access to public transportation

____ in a safe area

____ has outdoor lighting

____ is accessible to the handicapped

____ has comfortable seating

____ has a pleasant atmosphere

____ has kitchen facilities

Write down any other factors that will affect where you choose to hold your meetings:

_____

_____

It needs to be large enough to hold (number) _____ of people.

[Persons' Name(s)] _____ , _____ ,

_____ will check out the following facilities:

_____

_____

_____

You will need to think about or discuss how you are going to get people to come to the group. Some of your options include the following:

- Each person who is working on setting up the group invites several friends or other people they know by personal invitation, phone calls, mailing a note, or sending an email.

- Put a notice of the first meeting in the local newspaper or newspapers.

- Ask your local radio station or stations to announce it as a public service announcement.

- Ask for your meeting to be listed on your local community access television bulletin board.

- Hang posters describing the group in places where interested people might congregate (for example, if it is a group for people with a particular illness, you might put up posters in doctors' offices and hospital waiting rooms).

- Call people or send notices to those who might know others who might like to attend such a group.

Write down any other ideas you may have for how to find members for your group:

_____

_____

_____

The people starting the group will want to include all of the group members in making decisions about various aspects of the group's meetings. In one of the earliest meetings, the group will want to talk about and make mutual decisions regarding where the group will be held (if it is not going to meet where the initial meeting or meetings take place); how often it will meet; what time of day the meetings should happen; and how long the meetings should last. Questions about refreshments, the safety contract, the format of the group, and any other possible issues or concerns of the group members should be discussed and decided upon at the early meetings.

Although most groups meet weekly to maintain the continuity of the connection, your group could meet several times a week, every other week, or once a month.

This group will meet (check off those answers that apply):

_____ weekly (when) _____

_____ several times a week (when) _____

_____ every other week (when) _____

_____ once a month (when) _____

_____ other (when) _____

Most support groups meet in the evening. However, it is possible to hold meetings at any time that is the most convenient for the members.

This group will meet:

____ in the evening (when) _____

____ in the morning (when) _____

____ at noon _____

____ in the afternoon (when)_____

Depending on the time of day you are meeting, the length of the meetings, and the preference of the group members, you may want to have refreshments at the meetings, or even a potluck dinner. You may want to hold your meetings during breakfast, lunch, or dinner. Some people like to have something to munch on at meetings that are not held at meal times. Others may find this too distracting. Discuss this issue with group members. Take a vote if necessary.

Does the group want to have refreshments at the meetings? ____ y ____ n

Some options for handling refreshments include the following:

- Serve coffee and tea and have group members make donations to cover the costs.

- Have members take turns bringing light refreshments—the group may decide to request that no "junk foods" be served.

- One person purchases the refreshments for each meeting and members share the costs.

- Have refreshments occasionally or only at meetings that are near holidays or other celebrations.

- Have a pot luck dinner where everyone brings food to share: ____ at each meeting, or ____ only occasionally.

- Dine together at a restaurant: ____ at each meeting, or ____ only occasionally.

Developing a Safety Contract

A woman who started a very successful support group says, "The support group rules insist on confidentiality and no vulgarity. The meetings are nonconfrontational, and no one can monopolize the conversation. Although there are sometimes educational programs, the most important thing is *sharing*. It has taught me not to get too involved in other people's problems. If they ask for help I suggest something. If they don't follow my advice I have no problem. I am not one to say 'I told you so.'"

If you are going to attend a support group and connect with the other people in the group, everyone present must feel safe there. Many groups address this need by having a set of guidelines or rules for the group—sometimes called a safety contract. At one of the first group meetings, the members can discuss what they need in order to feel safe in the group. Although this contract varies from group to group depending on the group's purpose and focus, the following list describes some of the most common needs.

- Confidentiality: There must be a clear understanding that personal information shared in the group will not be shared with anyone outside of the group meeting.

- Membership: Group members will not tell people outside of the group who attends the group.

- Interruptions: There will be no interrupting when a group member is speaking or sharing.

- Sharing: Everyone will get a chance to share.

- Not sharing: If a group member doesn't feel like talking or sharing, that will be okay with other group members.

- Judgments: Judging, criticizing, teasing, or put-downs will not be allowed.

- Feedback: Group members will give other group members feedback only when it is requested.

- Personal comfort: People may leave the group whenever they want or need to take care of personal needs, to be comfortable, or to attend to other responsibilities.

- Attendance: Attendance is optional.

Which of the above items would you need to feel comfortable in a support group?

_____

_____

What else would you need to feel comfortable in a support group?

_____

_____

Formats for support groups vary widely. The members of the support group decide what they want the meetings to be like. If things don't work well one way, the group can choose to do them another way. Which of the following scenarios most closely matches the way you would like your group to be.

Our group meets once a week in the evening—at 7 P.M. When people first arrive they "chitchat" and drink tea until about 7:15 when the meeting is called to order by the person who volunteered to be the facilitator at this week's meeting. Then each person (there are ten people in our group) gets up to ten minutes to talk about the topic that was decided on by the group at the last meeting or anything else they might want to talk about that feels more pressing at the moment. The facilitator is also the timekeeper and warns people with hand signals when their time is up.

Because our support group is also a play group for young children, we meet in the morning, every other Friday. Either one or both parents attend. While the children play, we sit around and talk about whatever feels most important to us at the time.

Everyone in our group has multiple sclerosis. Sometimes we have speakers come to the beginning of our meetings, teaching us about the disease and introducing us to new forms of treatment and self-help strategies. They speak for about forty-five minutes on topics requested by the membership. For the rest of the time, each person shares for five minutes.

What kind of format would you like your support group to have?

_____

_____

_____

APPENDIX B

Peer Counseling Instructions

Peer counseling is a structured way to share the intimate details of your life. It can help you express your feelings, understand your problems, discover some helpful action you can take, and even to feel better. When used consistently, it is a free, safe, and effective self-help tool.

Peer counseling also provides you with an opportunity to give support to someone else and hear the details of his or her life. This helps to build closer relationships. Both aspects of peer counseling will help you to feel better. This form of counseling provides an opportunity to express yourself in any way you choose, while supported by a trusted friend. One woman described her peer counseling in this way: "I spend at least one afternoon a week peer counseling with a close friend. We have been doing this for about four years. I always look forward to it. It's a special time for both of us and helps relieve stress in our busy lives. Recently when I found myself feeling overwhelmed with worry about one of my children, I called my friend and arranged some extra peer counseling time."

Peer counseling is not the same as working with a professional counselor or therapist. Counselors and therapists have special skills and experience they use to help you deal with the troublesome issues in your life. A peer counselor provides only listening and does not give advice. But peer counseling is not the same as conversation. In a conversation, two or more people get together to discuss issues and experiences of mutual interest. There is no attempt made to ensure equal time, and there is a give-and-take in ordinary conversations that is not part of peer counseling.

In a peer counseling session, two people who like and trust each other agree to spend a previously agreed-upon amount of time together, dividing the time equally, to address and pay attention to each other's issues. For instance, if you have decided you will spend an hour together, the first half hour will be focused on one person and the second half hour on the other person. Sessions can be as short or as long as the two participants would like them to be. Often the length of time is predetermined by the demands of busy lives and hectic schedules. You can do it for ten minutes, with each person getting five minutes to talk and five minutes to listen—or for three hours, where each person gets one and a half hours to talk and one and a half hours to listen. Each format can be powerful and effective in its own way. Most people choose to do peer counseling for one hour, with each person sharing for half an hour.

It is understood that the content of these sessions is strictly confidential. Information that a person shares in a session is never to be shared with anyone else. Judging, criticizing, and advice-giving by the listener are not allowed. When the person speaking is using his or her time to be heard, the listener should make only an occasional neutral comment such as "I understand," "I'm sorry you are having such a hard time," or "I am here for you."

Sessions are held in a comfortable, quiet place where there will be no interruptions or distractions, and where the session cannot be overheard by others. Disconnect the phone, turn off the radio and television, find someone to watch small children, and do whatever else is necessary to eliminate distractions. Although most people prefer peer counseling sessions where we meet in person, they also can be held over the phone, when necessary.

The content of each session is determined by the person who is speaking or receiving attention—the "talker." The talker can use his or her time anyway he or she chooses. It may include eager talk, reluctant talk, tears, crying, trembling, ranting, indignant storming, laughter, yawning, shaking, singing, or punching a pillow.

As the talker, you may find it useful to focus on one issue and keep coming back to it despite any feelings you may have of wanting to avoid it. At other times, you may find yourself switching from subject to subject. At the beginning of a session, you may want to focus on one particular issue, but as you proceed, you may find other issues coming up that take precedence. All of this is up to you.. The person who listens and pays attention does only that. The listener must be an attentive, supportive listener.

At the beginning of a session, the listener can ask the talker to share several good things that have happened in the last week (or day, or month, etc.). This provides a positive starting point for the session. At the end of the session, the person who is listening can ask the person who is speaking to share something he or she is looking forward to.

In peer counseling, the expression of emotion is never *seen as a "symptom." Some people feel that strongly expressing an emotion means that something is wrong with you rather than viewing emotional expression as a vital part of being emotionally healthy. In the past, you may have been treated inappropriately for expressing a strong emotion. Consequently, you may have learned not to express your emotions because it is not safe, thus interfering with your emotional health. In peer counseling, you are encouraged to express your emotions.*

Many people find that, when they first try peer counseling, it is very difficult to:

- find enough to say or to share when it is your time

- avoid interrupting the other person

- avoid giving feedback or advice

With practice, however, all of these things will become easier for you.

It is a good idea when you first begin peer counseling to try doing it only for ten minutes—five minutes for each person. As you feel more comfortable with the process, you can lengthen your sessions to last for longer and longer periods of time.

APPENDIX C

Resources

The following list contains resources that may be helpful to you as you work to relieve your loneliness. You can find many other resources through your library, bookstores, and on the Internet.

Anger

Lerner, H. 1985. *The Dance of Anger*. New York: Harper & Row.

McKay, M., P. Rogers, and J. McKay. 1989. *When Anger Hurts*. Oakland, CA: New Harbinger Publications.

Anxiety

Bourne, E. 1995. *The Anxiety & Phobia Workbook*. Second Edition. Oakland, CA: New Harbinger Publications.

Bourne, E. 1998. *Healing Fear: New Approaches to Overcoming Anxiety*. Oakland, CA: New Harbinger Publications.

Copeland, M.E. 1998. *The Worry Control Workbook*. Oakland, CA: New Harbinger Publications.

Changing Negative Thoughts to Positive Ones

Burns, D. 1989. *The Feeling Good Handbook*. New York: W. Morrow.

Family Issues

Lauer, J., and R. Lauer. 1999. *How To Survive and Thrive in an Empty Nest: Reclaiming your Life When Your Children have Grown*. Oakland, CA: New Harbinger Publications.

Brown, E.M. 1994. *Stepfamily Realities: How to Overcome Difficulties and Have a Happy Family*. Oakland, CA: New Harbinger Publications.

Gay and Lesbian Issues

Hardin, K. 1999. *The Gay and Lesbian Self-Esteem Book: A Guide to Loving Ourselves*. Oakland, CA: New Harbinger Publications.

Loss and Grief

Harris, M. 1995. *The Loss That Is Forever: The Lifelong Impact of the Early Death of a Mother or Father*. New York: Dutton.

Grotberg, E. 1999. *Tapping Your Inner Strength: How to Find the Resilience to Deal with Anything*. Oakland, CA: New Harbinger Publications.

Staudacher, C. 1987. *Beyond Grief: A Guide for Recovering from the Death of a Loved One*. Oakland, CA: New Harbinger Publications.

Mental Health and Wellness

Copeland, M. 1999. *Winning Against Relapse*. Oakland, CA: New Harbinger Publications.

Copeland, M. 1992. *The Depression Workbook: A Guide to Living with Depression and Manic Depression*. Oakland, CA: New Harbinger Publications.

Copeland, M. 1994. *Living without Depression and Manic Depression*. Oakland, CA: New Harbinger Publications.

Karp, D. 1996. *Speaking of Sadness: Depression, Disconnection, and the Meaning of Illness*. New York: Oxford University Press

Slagle, P. 1988. *The Way Up From Down*. New York: St. Martin's Press.

Relationships

Burns, D. 1985. *Intimate Connections*. New York: W. Morrow.

Hendrix, H. 1988. *Getting The Love You Want: A Guide for Couples*. New York: Harper Perennial.

Woititz, J.G. 1985. *Struggle for Intimacy*. Pompano Beach, FL: Health Communications.

Relaxation and Stress Reduction

Davis, M., Eschelman, E. and M. McKay. 1995. *The Relaxation and Stress Reduction Workbook,* Fourth Edition. Oakland, CA: New Harbinger Publications.

Kabat-Zinn, J. 1990. *Full Catastrophe Living*. New York: Delacorte Press.

McKay, M. 1997. *The Daily Relaxer*. Oakland, CA: New Harbinger Publications.

Self-Esteem and Personal Empowerment

Miller, T. 1998. *Wanting What you Have: A Self-Discovery Workbook*. Oakland, CA: New Harbinger Publications

Rutledge, T. 1997. *The Self-Forgiveness Handbook: A Practical and Empowering Guide*. Oakland, CA: New Harbinger Publications.

McKay, M., and P. Fanning. 1993. *Self-Esteem* (Second Edition). Oakland, CA: New Harbinger Publications.

McKay, M., P. Fanning, C. Honeychurch, and C. Sutker. 1999. *The Self-Esteem Companion*. Oakland, CA: New Harbinger Publications.

McDermott, D., and C.R. Snyder. 1999. *Making Hope Happen: A Workbook for Turning Possibilities into Reality*. Oakland, CA: New Harbinger Publications.

Social Skills

Affinito, M. G. 1999. *When To Forgive*. Oakland, CA: New Harbinger Publications.

Kahn, M. 1995. *The Tao of Conversation*. Oakland, CA: New Harbinger Publications.

McKay, M., M. Davis, and P. Fanning. 1995. *Messages: The Communication Skills Book*. Second Edition. Oakland, CA: New Harbinger Publications.

Potter-Efron, R. 1998. *Being, Belonging, Doing: Balancing Your Three Greatest Needs*. Oakland, CA: New Harbinger Publications.

Savage, E. 1997. *Don't Take It Personally! The Art of Dealing with Rejection*. Oakland, CA: New Harbinger Publications.

Web Sites

Mary Ellen Copeland, http://www.mentalhealthrecovery.com and http://www.maryellencopeland.com.

Seminars

Mary Ellen Copeland leads several five-day seminars throughout the year. To get more information on these seminars, contact her through the web site at www.mentalhealthrecovery.com, call (802) 254-2092 or email her at copeland@mentalhealthrecovery.com.

References

The American Heritage Dictionary of the English Language. 1992. New York: Houghton Mifflin Co.

Burns, D. 1985. *Intimate Connections*. New York: Morrow.

Copeland, M. E. *The Depression Workbook*. 1999. Oakland, CA: New Harbinger Publications.

———. 1999. *Winning Against Relapse*. Oakland, CA: New Harbinger Publications.

———. 1994. *Living Without Depression and Manic Depression*. Oakland, CA: New Harbinger Publications.

Mackay, M., M. Davis, and P. Fanning. 1995. *Messages: The Communication Skills Book*. Oakland, CA: New Harbinger Publications.

Saint-Exupéry, Antoine de. 1943. *The Little Prince*. New York: Harcourt, Brace, & World.

More tools for change from Mary Ellen Copeland

WINNING AGAINST RELAPSE

Helps anyone recovering from an illness or struggling with a chronic physical or emotional problem reduce or eliminate the possiblity of relapse.
Item WIN $14.95

THE WORRY CONTROL WORKBOOK

Helps you identify areas where specific types of worry are likely to reoccur and develop new skills for dealing with them.
Item WCW $15.95

THE DEPRESSION WORKBOOK

Teaches essential coping skills, such as building a strong support system, bolstering self-esteem, fighting negative thoughts, and finding appropriate professional help.
Item DEP $18.95

LIVING WITHOUT DEPRESSION AND MANIC DEPRESSION

Covers self-advocacy, wellness lifestyle, dealing with sleep problems, finding a career that works, and much more.
Item MOOD $18.95

COPING WITH DEPRESSION

This 60-minute video enriches the advice and techniques contained in Mary Ellen's books with explanations and vivid examples presented to a live audience.
Item 501 (VHS only) $39.95

LIVING WITH DEPRESSION AND MANIC DEPRESSION

Inspires confidence that you can achieve real breakthroughs in coping with depression or manic depression. One cassette in a rigid plastic box.
Item 41 $11.95

Call **toll-free 1-800-748-6273** to order. Have your Visa or Mastercard number ready. Or send a check for the titles you want to New Harbinger Publications, 5674 Shattuck Avenue, Oakland, CA 94609. Include $3.80 for the first book and 75¢ for each additional book to cover shipping and handling. (California residents please include appropriate sales tax.) Allow four to six weeks for delivery.

Prices subject to change without notice.

Some Other New Harbinger Self-Help Titles

Family Guide to Emotional Wellness, $24.95
Undefended Love, $13.95
The Great Big Book of Hope, $15.95
Don't Leave it to Chance, $13.95
Emotional Claustrophobia, $12.95
The Relaxation & Stress Reduction Workbook, Fifth Edition, $19.95
The Loneliness Workbook, $14.95
Thriving with Your Autoimmune Disorder, $16.95
Illness and the Art of Creative Self-Expression, $13.95
The Interstitial Cystitis Survival Guide, $14.95
Outbreak Alert, $15.95
Don't Let Your Mind Stunt Your Growth, $10.95
Energy Tapping, $14.95
Under Her Wing, $13.95
Self-Esteem, Third Edition, $15.95
Women's Sexualitites, $15.95
Knee Pain, $14.95
Helping Your Anxious Child, $12.95
Breaking the Bonds of Irritable Bowel Syndrome, $14.95
Multiple Chemical Sensitivity: A Survival Guide, $16.95
Dancing Naked, $14.95
Why Are We Still Fighting, $15.95
From Sabotage to Success, $14.95
Parkinson's Disease and the Art of Moving, $15.95
A Survivor's Guide to Breast Cancer, $13.95
Men, Women, and Prostate Cancer, $15.95
Make Every Session Count: Getting the Most Out of Your Brief Therapy, $10.95
Virtual Addiction, $12.95
After the Breakup, $13.95
Why Can't I Be the Parent I Want to Be?, $12.95
The Secret Message of Shame, $13.95
The OCD Workbook, $18.95
Tapping Your Inner Strength, $13.95
Binge No More, $14.95
When to Forgive, $12.95
Practical Dreaming, $12.95
Healthy Baby, Toxic World, $15.95
Making Hope Happen, $14.95
I'll Take Care of You, $12.95
Survivor Guilt, $14.95
Children Changed by Trauma, $13.95
Understanding Your Child's Sexual Behavior, $12.95
The Self-Esteem Companion, $10.95
The Gay and Lesbian Self-Esteem Book, $13.95
Making the Big Move, $13.95
How to Survive and Thrive in an Empty Nest, $13.95
Living Well with a Hidden Disability, $15.95
Overcoming Repetitive Motion Injuries the Rossiter Way, $15.95
What to Tell the Kids About Your Divorce, $13.95
The Divorce Book, Second Edition, $15.95
Claiming Your Creative Self: True Stories from the Everyday Lives of Women, $15.95
Taking Control of TMJ, $13.95
What You Need to Know About Alzheimer's, $15.95
Winning Against Relapse: A Workbook of Action Plans for Recurring Health and Emotional Problems, $14.95
Facing 30: Women Talk About Constructing a Real Life and Other Scary Rites of Passage, $12.95
The Worry Control Workbook, $15.95
Wanting What You Have: A Self-Discovery Workbook, $18.95
When Perfect Isn't Good Enough: Strategies for Coping with Perfectionism, $13.95
Earning Your Own Respect: A Handbook of Personal Responsibility, $12.95
High on Stress: A Woman's Guide to Optimizing the Stress in Her Life, $13.95
Infidelity: A Survival Guide, $13.95
Stop Walking on Eggshells, $14.95
Consumer's Guide to Psychiatric Drugs, $16.95
The Fibromyalgia Advocate: Getting the Support You Need to Cope with Fibromyalgia and Myofascial Pain, $18.95
Working Anger: Preventing and Resolving Conflict on the Job, $12.95
Healthy Living with Diabetes, $13.95
Better Boundries: Owning and Treasuring Your Life, $13.95
Goodbye Good Girl, $12.95
Fibromyalgia & Chronic Myofascial Pain Syndrome, $19.95
The Depression Workbook: Living With Depression and Manic Depression, $17.95
Angry All the Time: An Emergency Guide to Anger Control, $12.95

Call **toll free, 1-800-748-6273,** or log on to our online bookstore at **www.newharbinger.com** to order. Have your Visa or Mastercard number ready. Or send a check for the titles you want to New Harbinger Publications, Inc., 5674 Shattuck Ave., Oakland, CA 94609. Include $3.80 for the first book and 75¢ for each additional book, to cover shipping and handling. (California residents please include appropriate sales tax.) Allow two to five weeks for delivery.

Prices subject to change without notice.